Test-Driven Development

The Addison-Wesley Signature Series

The Addison-Wesley Signature Series provides readers with practical and authoritative information on the latest trends in modern technology for computer professionals. The series is based on one simple premise: great books come from great authors. Books in the series are personally chosen by expert advisors, world-class authors in their own right. These experts are proud to put their signatures on the covers, and their signatures ensure that these thought leaders have worked closely with authors to define topic coverage, book scope, critical content, and overall uniqueness. The expert signatures also symbolize a promise to our readers: you are reading a future classic.

THE ADDISON–WESLEY SIGNATURE SERIES
SIGNERS: KENT BECK & MARTIN FOWLER

Martin Fowler has been a pioneer of object technology in enterprise applications. His central concern is how to design software well. He focuses on getting to the heart of how to build enterprise software that will last well into the future. He is interested in looking behind the specifics of technologies to the patterns, practices, and principles that last for many years; these books should be usable a decade from now. Martin's criterion is that these are books he wished he could write.

Kent Beck has pioneered people-oriented technologies like JUnit, Extreme Programming, and patterns for software development. Kent is interested in helping teams do well by doing good – finding a style of software development that simultaneously satisfies economic, aesthetic, emotional, and practical constraints. His books focus on touching the lives of the creators and users of software.

TITLES IN THE SERIES

Patterns of Enterprise Application Architecture
Martin Fowler, ISBN: 0321127420

Beyond Software Architecture: Creating and Sustaining Winning Solutions
Luke Hohmann, ISBN: 0201775948

Test-Driven Development: By Example
Kent Beck, ISBN: 0321146530

For more information, check out the series Web site at http://www.awprofessional.com/

Test-Driven Development

By Example

Kent Beck

✦Addison-Wesley

Boston • San Francisco • New York • Toronto • Montreal
London • Munich • Paris • Madrid
Capetown • Sydney • Tokyo • Singapore • Mexico City

Many of the designations used by manufacturers and sellers to distinguish their products are claimed as trademarks. Where those designations appear in this book, and Addison-Wesley was aware of a trademark claim, the designations have been printed with initial capital letters or in all capitals.

The author and publisher have taken care in the preparation of this book, but make no expressed or implied warranty of any kind and assume no responsibility for errors or omissions. No liability is assumed for incidental or consequential damages in connection with or arising out of the use of the information or programs contained herein.

The publisher offers discounts on this book when ordered in quantity for bulk purchases and special sales. For more information, please contact:

U.S. Corporate and Government Sales
(800) 382-3419
corpsales@pearsontechgroup.com

For sales outside of the U.S., please contact:

International Sales
(317) 581-3793
international@pearsontechgroup.com

Visit Addison-Wesley on the Web: www.awprofessional.com

Library of Congress Cataloging-in-Publication Data

Beck, Kent.
    Test-driven development : by example / Kent Beck.
        p. cm.
    Includes index.
    ISBN 0-321-14653-0 (alk. paper)
    1. Computer software—Testing.   2. Computer software—Development.   3. Computer programming.   I. Title.

QA76.76.T48 B43 2003
005.1'4—dc21

                                                                    2002028037

Pearson Education, Inc.
Rights and Contracts Department
75 Arlington Street, Suite 300
Boston, MA 02116
Fax: (617) 848-7047

ISBN 0-321-14653-0
Text printed on recycled paper
1 2 3 4 5 6 7 8 9 10—CRS—0605040302
First printing, October 2002

To Cindee: wings of your own

Contents

Preface

Clean code that works, in Ron Jeffries' pithy phrase, is the goal of Test-Driven Development (TDD). Clean code that works is a worthwhile goal for a whole bunch of reasons.

- It is a predictable way to develop. You know when you are finished, without having to worry about a long bug trail.

- It gives you a chance to learn all of the lessons that the code has to teach you. If you only slap together the first thing you think of, then you never have time to think of a second, better thing.

- It improves the lives of the users of your software.

- It lets your teammates count on you, and you on them.

- It feels good to write it.

But how do we get to clean code that works? Many forces drive us away from clean code, and even from code that works. Without taking too much counsel of our fears, here's what we do: we drive development with automated tests, a style of development called Test-Driven Development (TDD). In Test-Driven Development, we

- Write new code only if an automated test has failed

- Eliminate duplication

These are two simple rules, but they generate complex individual and group behavior with technical implications such as the following.

- We must design organically, with running code providing feedback between decisions.

- We must write our own tests, because we can't wait 20 times per day for someone else to write a test.

- Our development environment must provide rapid response to small changes.

- Our designs must consist of many highly cohesive, loosely coupled components, just to make testing easy.

The two rules imply an order to the tasks of programming.

1. Red—Write a little test that doesn't work, and perhaps doesn't even compile at first.

2. Green—Make the test work quickly, committing whatever sins necessary in the process.

3. Refactor—Eliminate all of the duplication created in merely getting the test to work.

Red/green/refactor—the TDD mantra.

Assuming for the moment that such a programming style is possible, it further might be possible to dramatically reduce the defect density of code and make the subject of work crystal clear to all involved. If so, then writing only that code which is demanded by failing tests also has social implications.

- If the defect density can be reduced enough, then quality assurance (QA) can shift from reactive work to proactive work.

- If the number of nasty surprises can be reduced enough, then project managers can estimate accurately enough to involve real customers in daily development.

- If the topics of technical conversations can be made clear enough, then software engineers can work in minute-by-minute collaboration instead of daily or weekly collaboration.

- Again, if the defect density can be reduced enough, then we can have shippable software with new functionality every day, leading to new business relationships with customers.

So the concept is simple, but what's my motivation? Why would a software engineer take on the additional work of writing automated tests? Why would a software engineer work in tiny little steps when his or her mind is capable of great soaring swoops of design? Courage.

Courage

Test-driven development is a way of managing fear during programming. I don't mean fear in a bad way—*pow widdle prwogwammew needs a pacifiew*—but fear in the legitimate, this-is-a-hard-problem-and-I-can't-see-the-end-from-the-beginning sense. If pain is nature's way of saying "Stop!" then fear is nature's way of saying "Be careful." Being careful is good, but fear has a host of other effects.

- Fear makes you tentative.

- Fear makes you want to communicate less.

- Fear makes you shy away from feedback.

- Fear makes you grumpy.

None of these effects are helpful when programming, especially when programming something hard. So the question becomes how we face a difficult situation and,

- Instead of being tentative, begin learning concretely as quickly as possible.

- Instead of clamming up, communicate more clearly.

- Instead of avoiding feedback, search out helpful, concrete feedback.

- (You'll have to work on grumpiness on your own.)

Imagine programming as turning a crank to pull a bucket of water from a well. When the bucket is small, a free-spinning crank is fine. When the bucket is big and full of water, you're going to get tired before the bucket is all the way up. You need a ratchet mechanism to enable you to rest between bouts of cranking. The heavier the bucket, the closer the teeth need to be on the ratchet.

The tests in test-driven development are the teeth of the ratchet. Once we get one test working, we know it is working, now and forever. We are one step closer to having everything working than we were when the test was broken. Now we get the next one working, and the next, and the next. By analogy, the tougher the programming problem, the less ground that each test should cover.

Readers of my book *Extreme Programming Explained* will notice a difference in tone between Extreme Programming (XP) and TDD. TDD isn't an absolute the way that XP is. XP says, "Here are things you must be able to do to be prepared to evolve further." TDD is a little fuzzier. TDD is an awareness of the gap between decision and feedback during programming, and techniques to control that gap. "What if I do a paper design for a week, then test-drive the code? Is that TDD?" Sure, it's TDD. You were aware of the gap between decision and feedback, and you controlled the gap deliberately.

That said, most people who learn TDD find that their programming practice changed for good. *Test Infected* is the phrase Erich Gamma coined to describe this shift. You might find yourself writing more tests earlier, and working in smaller steps than you ever dreamed would be sensible. On the other hand, some software engineers learn TDD and then revert to their earlier practices, reserving TDD for special occasions when ordinary programming isn't making progress.

There certainly are programming tasks that can't be driven solely by tests (or at least, not yet). Security software and concurrency, for example, are two topics where TDD is insufficient to mechanically demonstrate that the goals of the software have been met. Although it's true that security relies on essentially defect-free code, it also relies on human judgment about the methods used to secure the software. Subtle concurrency problems can't be reliably duplicated by running the code.

Once you are finished reading this book, you should be ready to

- Start simply

- Write automated tests

- Refactor to add design decisions one at a time

This book is organized in three parts.

- Part I, The Money Example—An example of typical model code written using TDD. The example is one I got from Ward Cunningham years ago and have used many times since: multi-currency arithmetic. This example will enable you to learn to write tests before code and grow a design organically.

- Part II, The xUnit Example—An example of testing more complicated logic, including reflection and exceptions, by developing a framework for automated testing. This example also will introduce you to the xUnit architecture that is at the heart of many programmer-oriented testing tools. In the second example, you will learn to work in even smaller steps than in the first example, including the kind of self-referential hoo-ha beloved of computer scientists.

- Part III, Patterns for Test-Driven Development—Included are patterns for deciding what tests to write, how to write tests using xUnit, and a greatest-hits selection of the design patterns and refactorings used in the examples.

I wrote the examples imagining a pair programming session. If you like looking at the map before wandering around, then you may want to go straight to the patterns in Part III and use the examples as illustrations. If you prefer just wandering around and then looking at the map to see where you've been, then try reading through the examples, referring to the patterns when you want more detail about a technique, and using the patterns as a reference. Several reviewers of this book commented they got the most out of the examples when they started up a programming environment, entered the code, and ran the tests as they read.

A note about the examples. Both of the examples, multi-currency calculation and a testing framework, appear simple. There are (and I have seen) complicated, ugly, messy ways of solving the same problems. I could have chosen one of those complicated, ugly, messy solutions, to give the book an air of "reality." However, my goal, and I hope your goal, is to write clean code that works. Before teeing off on the examples as being too simple, spend 15 seconds imagining a programming world in which all code was this clear and direct, where there were no complicated solutions, only apparently complicated problems begging for careful thought. TDD can help you to lead yourself to exactly that careful thought.

Acknowledgments

Thanks to all of my many brutal and opinionated reviewers. I take full responsibility for the contents, but this book would have been much less readable and much less useful without their help. In the order in which I typed them, they were: Steve Freeman, Frank Westphal, Ron Jeffries, Dierk König, Edward Hieatt, Tammo Freese, Jim Newkirk, Johannes Link, Manfred Lange, Steve Hayes, Alan Francis, Jonathan Rasmusson, Shane Clauson, Simon Crase, Kay Pentecost, Murray Bishop, Ryan King, Bill Wake, Edmund Schweppe, Kevin Lawrence, John Carter, Phlip, Peter Hansen, Ben Schroeder, Alex Chaffee, Peter van Rooijen, Rick Kawala, Mark van Hamersveld, Doug Swartz, Laurent Bossavit, Ilja Preuß, Daniel Le Berre, Frank Carver, Justin Sampson, Mike Clark, Christian Pekeler, Karl Scotland, Carl Manaster, J. B. Rainsberger, Peter Lindberg, Darach Ennis, Kyle Cordes, Justin Sampson, Patrick Logan, Darren Hobbs, Aaron Sansone, Syver Enstad, Shinobu Kawai, Erik Meade, Patrick Logan, Dan Rawsthorne, Bill Rutiser, Eric Herman, Paul Chisholm, Asim Jalis, Ivan Moore, Levi Purvis, Rick Mugridge, Anthony Adachi, Nigel Thorne, John Bley, Kari Hoijarvi, Manuel Amago, Kaoru Hosokawa, Pat Eyler, Ross Shaw, Sam Gentle, Jean Rajotte, Phillipe Antras, and Jaime Nino.

To all of the programmers I've test-driven code with, I certainly appreciate your patience going along with what was a pretty crazy sounding idea, especially in the early years. I've learned far more from you all than I could ever think of myself. Not wishing to offend everyone else, but Massimo Arnoldi, Ralph Beattie, Ron Jeffries, Martin Fowler, and last but certainly not least Erich Gamma stand out in my memory as test drivers from whom I've learned much.

I would like to thank Martin Fowler for timely FrameMaker help. He must be the highest-paid typesetting consultant on the planet, but fortunately he has let me (so far) run a tab.

My life as a real programmer started with patient mentoring from and continuing collaboration with Ward Cunningham. Sometimes I see Test-Driven

Development (TDD) as an attempt to give any software engineer, working in any environment, the sense of comfort and intimacy we had with our Smalltalk environment and our Smalltalk programs. There is no way to sort out the source of ideas once two people have shared a brain. If you assume that all of the good ideas here are Ward's, then you won't be far wrong.

It is a bit cliché to recognize the sacrifices a family makes once one of its members catches the peculiar mental affliction that results in a book. That's because family sacrifices are as necessary to book writing as paper is. To my children, who waited breakfast until I could finish a chapter, and most of all to my wife, who spent two months saying everything three times, my most-profound and least-adequate thanks.

Thanks to Mike Henderson for gentle encouragement and to Marcy Barnes for riding to the rescue.

Finally, to the unknown author of the book which I read as a weird 12-year-old that suggested you type in the expected output tape from a real input tape, then code until the actual results matched the expected result, thank you, thank you, thank you.

Introduction

Early one Friday, the boss came to Ward Cunningham to introduce him to Peter, a prospective customer for WyCash, the bond portfolio management system the company was selling. Peter said, "I'm very impressed with the functionality I see. However, I notice you only handle U.S. dollar denominated bonds. I'm starting a new bond fund, and my strategy requires that I handle bonds in different currencies." The boss turned to Ward, "Well, can we do it?"

Here is the nightmarish scenario for any software designer. You were cruising along happily and successfully with a set of assumptions. Suddenly, everything changed. And the nightmare wasn't just for Ward. The boss, an experienced hand at directing software development, wasn't sure what the answer was going to be.

A small team had developed WyCash over the course of a couple of years. The system was able to handle most of the varieties of fixed income securities commonly found on the U.S. market, and a few exotic new instruments, like Guaranteed Investment Contracts, that the competition couldn't handle.

WyCash had been developed all along using objects and an object database. The fundamental abstraction of computation, Dollar, had been outsourced at the beginning to a clever group of software engineers. The resulting object combined formatting and calculation responsibilities.

For the past six months, Ward and the rest of the team had been slowly divesting Dollar of its responsibilities. The Smalltalk numerical classes turned out to be just fine at calculation. All of the tricky code for rounding to three decimal digits got in the way of producing precise answers. As the answers became more precise, the complicated mechanisms in the testing framework for comparison within a certain tolerance were replaced by precise matching of expected and actual results.

Responsibility for formatting actually belonged in the user interface classes. As the tests were written at the level of the user interface classes, in particular the report framework,[1] these tests didn't have to change to accommodate this refinement. After six months of careful paring, the resulting Dollar didn't have much responsibility left.

One of the most complicated algorithms in the system, weighted average, likewise had been undergoing a slow transformation. At one time, there had been many different variations of weighted average code scattered throughout the system. As the report framework coalesced from the primordial object soup, it was obvious that there could be one home for the algorithm, in AveragedColumn.

It was to AveragedColumn that Ward now turned. If weighted averages could be made multi-currency, then the rest of the system should be possible. At the heart of the algorithm was keeping a count of the money in the column. In fact, the algorithm had been abstracted enough to calculate the weighted average of any object that could act arithmetically. One could have weighted averages of dates, for example.

The weekend passed with the usual weekend activities. Monday morning the boss was back. "Can we do it?"

"Give me another day, and I'll tell you for sure."

Dollar acted like a counter in weighted average; therefore, in order to calculate in multiple currencies, they needed an object with a counter per currency, kind of like a polynomial. Instead of $3x^2$ and $4y^3$, however, the terms would be 15 USD and 200 CHF.

A quick experiment showed that it was possible to compute with a generic Currency object instead of a Dollar, and return a PolyCurrency when two unlike currencies were added together. The trick now was to make space for the new functionality without breaking anything that already worked. What would happen if Ward just ran the tests?

After the addition of a few unimplemented operations to Currency, the bulk of the tests passed. By the end of the day, all of the tests were passing. Ward checked the code into the build and went to the boss. "We can do it," he said confidently.

Let's think a bit about this story. In two days, the potential market was multiplied several fold, multiplying the value of WyCash several fold. The ability to create so much business value so quickly was no accident, however. Several factors came into play.

- Method—Ward and the WyCash team needed to have constant experience growing the design of the system, little by little, so the mechanics of the transformation were well practiced.

---

1. For more about the report framework, refer to c2.com/doc/oopsla91.html.

- Motive—Ward and his team needed to understand clearly the business importance of making WyCash multi-currency, and to have the courage to start such a seemingly impossible task.

- Opportunity—The combination of comprehensive, confidence-generating tests; a well-factored program; and a programming language that made it possible to isolate design decisions meant that there were few sources of error, and those errors were easy to identify.

You can't control whether you ever get the motive to multiply the value of your project by spinning technical magic. Method and opportunity, on the other hand, are entirely under your control. Ward and his team created method and opportunity through a combination of superior talent, experience, and discipline. Does this mean that if you are not one of the ten best software engineers on the planet and don't have a wad of cash in the bank so you can tell your boss to take a hike, then you're going to take the time to do this right, that such moments are forever beyond your reach?

No. You absolutely can place your projects in a position for you to work magic, even if you are a software engineer with ordinary skills and you sometimes buckle under and take shortcuts when the pressure builds. Test-driven development is a set of techniques that any software engineer can follow, which encourages simple designs and test suites that inspire confidence. If you are a genius, you don't need these rules. If you are a dolt, the rules won't help. For the vast majority of us in between, following these two simple rules can lead us to work much more closely to our potential.

- Write a failing automated test before you write any code.

- Remove duplication.

How exactly to do this, the subtle gradations in applying these rules, and the lengths to which you can push these two simple rules are the topic of this book. We'll start with the object that Ward created in his moment of inspiration—multi-currency money.

PART I

The Money Example

In Part I, we will develop typical model code driven completely by tests (except when we slip, purely for educational purposes). My goal is for you to see the rhythm of Test-Driven Development (TDD), which can be summed up as follows.

1. Quickly add a test.

2. Run all tests and see the new one fail.

3. Make a little change.

4. Run all tests and see them all succeed.

5. Refactor to remove duplication.

The surprises are likely to include

- How each test can cover a small increment of functionality

- How small and ugly the changes can be to make the new tests run

- How often the tests are run

- How many teensy-weensy steps make up the refactorings

Chapter 1

Multi-Currency Money

We'll start with the object that Ward created at WyCash, multi-currency money (refer to the Introduction). Suppose we have a report like this:

Instrument	Shares	Price	Total
IBM	1000	25	25000
GE	400	100	40000
		Total	65000

To make a multi-currency report, we need to add currencies:

Instrument	Shares	Price	Total
IBM	1000	25 USD	25000 USD
Novartis	400	150 CHF	60000 CHF
		Total	65000 USD

We also need to specify exchange rates:

From	To	Rate
CHF	USD	1.5

$5 + 10 CHF = $10 if rate is 2:1
$5 * 2 = $10

What behavior will we need to produce the revised report? Put another way, what set of tests, when passed, will demonstrate the presence of code we are confident will compute the report correctly?

- We need to be able to add amounts in two different currencies and convert the result given a set of exchange rates.

- We need to be able to multiply an amount (price per share) by a number (number of shares) and receive an amount.

We'll make a to-do list to remind us what we need to do, to keep us focused, and to tell us when we are finished. When we start working on an item, we'll make it bold, **like this**. When we finish an item, we'll cross it off, ~~like this~~. When we think of another test to write, we'll add it to the list.

As you can see from the to-do list on the previous page, we'll work on multiplication first. So, what object do we need first? Trick question. We don't start with objects, we start with tests. (I keep having to remind myself of this, so I will pretend you are as dense as I am.)

Try again. What test do we need first? Looking at the list, that first test looks complicated. Start small or not at all. Multiplication, how hard could that be? We'll work on that first.

When we write a test, we imagine the perfect interface for our operation. We are telling ourselves a story about how the operation will look from the outside. Our story won't always come true, but it's better to start from the best-possible application program interface (API) and work backward than to make things complicated, ugly, and "realistic" from the get-go.

Here's a simple example of multiplication:

```
public void testMultiplication() {
    Dollar five= new Dollar(5);
    five.times(2);
    assertEquals(10, five.amount);
}
```

(I know, I know, public fields, side-effects, integers for monetary amounts, and all that. Small steps. We'll make a note of the stinkiness and move on. We have a failing test, and we want the bar to go to green as quickly as possible.)

$5 + 10 CHF = $10 if rate is 2:1
$5 * 2 = $10
Make "amount" private
Dollar side-effects?
Money rounding?

The test we just typed in doesn't even compile. (I'll explain where and how we type it in later, when we talk more about the testing framework, JUnit.) That's easy enough to fix. What's the least we can do to get it to compile, even if it doesn't run? We have four compile errors:

- No class Dollar
- No constructor
- No method times(int)
- No field amount

Let's take them one at a time. (I always search for some numerical measure of progress.) We can get rid of one error by defining the class Dollar:

Dollar
```
class Dollar
```

One error down, three errors to go. Now we need the constructor, but it doesn't have to do anything just to get the test to compile:

Dollar
```
Dollar(int amount) {
}
```

Two errors to go. We need a stub implementation of times(). Again we'll do the least work possible just to get the test to compile:

Dollar
```
void times(int multiplier) {
}
```

Down to one error. Finally, we need an amount field:

Dollar
```
int amount;
```

Bingo! Now we can run the test and watch it fail, as shown in Figure 1.1.

You are seeing the dreaded red bar. Our testing framework (JUnit, in this case) has run the little snippet of code we started with, and noticed that although we expected "10" as a result, instead we saw "0". Sadness.

No, no. Failure is progress. Now we have a concrete measure of failure. That's better than just vaguely knowing we are failing. Our programming problem has been transformed from "give me multi-currency" to "make this test work, and then make the rest of the tests work." Much simpler. Much smaller scope for fear. We can make this test work.

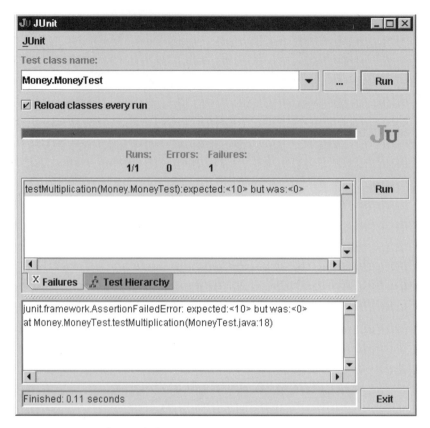

Figure 1.1 *Progress! The test fails*

You probably aren't going to like the solution, but the goal right now is not to get the perfect answer but to pass the test. We'll make our sacrifice at the altar of truth and beauty later.

Here's the smallest change I could imagine that would cause our test to pass:

Dollar

```
int amount= 10;
```

Figure 1.2 shows the result when the test is run again. Now we get the green bar, fabled in song and story

Oh joy, oh rapture! Not so fast, hacker boy (or girl). The cycle isn't complete. There are very few inputs in the world that will cause such a limited, such

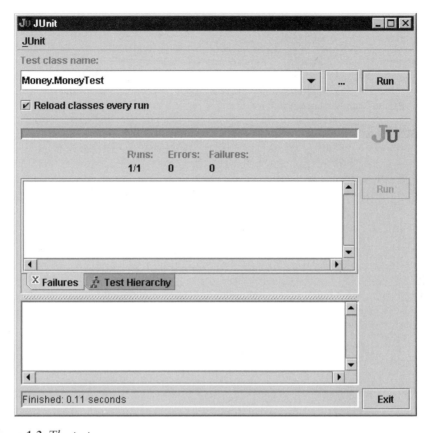

Figure 1.2 *The test runs*

a smelly, such a naïve implementation to pass. We need to generalize before we move on. Remember, the cycle is as follows.

1. Add a little test.

2. Run all tests and fail.

3. Make a little change.

4. Run the tests and succeed.

5. Refactor to remove duplication.

Dependency and Duplication

Steve Freeman pointed out that the problem with the test and code as it sits is not duplication (which I have not yet pointed out to you, but I promise to as soon as this digression is over). The problem is the dependency between the code and the test—you can't change one without changing the other. Our goal is to be able to write another test that "makes sense" to us, without having to change the code, something that is not possible with the current implementation.

Dependency is the key problem in software development at all scales. If you have details of one vendor's implementation of SQL scattered throughout the code and you decide to change to another vendor, then you will discover that your code is dependent on the database vendor. You can't change the database without changing the code.

If dependency is the problem, duplication is the symptom. Duplication most often takes the form of duplicate logic—the same expression appearing in multiple places in the code. Objects are excellent for abstracting away the duplication of logic.

Unlike most problems in life, where eliminating the symptoms only makes the problem pop up elsewhere in worse form, eliminating duplication in programs eliminates dependency. That's why the second rule appears in TDD. By eliminating duplication before we go on to the next test, we maximize our chance of being able to get the next test running with one and only one change.

We have run items 1 through 4. Now we are ready to remove duplication. But where is the duplication? Usually you see duplication between two pieces of code, but here the duplication is between the data in the test and the data in the code. Don't see it? How about if we write the following:

Dollar
```
int amount= 5 * 2;
```

That 10 had to come from somewhere. We did the multiplication in our heads so fast we didn't even notice. The 5 and 2 are now in two places, and we must ruthlessly eliminate duplication before moving on. The rules say so.

There isn't a single step that will eliminate the 5 and the 2. But what if we move the setting of the amount from object initialization to the times() method?

Dollar
```
int amount;

void times(int multiplier) {
   amount= 5 * 2;
}
```

The test still passes, the bar stays green. Happiness is still ours.

Do these steps seem too small to you? Remember, TDD is not about taking teeny-tiny steps, it's about *being able to* take teeny-tiny steps. Would I code day-to-day with steps this small? No. But when things get the least bit weird, I'm glad I can. Try teeny-tiny steps with an example of your own choosing. If you can make steps too small, you can certainly make steps the right size. If you only take larger steps, you'll never know if smaller steps are appropriate.

Defensiveness aside, where were we? Ah, yes, we were getting rid of duplication between the test code and the working code. Where can we get a 5? That was the value passed to the constructor, so if we save it in the amount variable,

Dollar
```
Dollar(int amount) {
   this.amount= amount;
}
```

then we can use it in `times()`:

Dollar
```
void times(int multiplier) {
   amount= amount * 2;
}
```

The value of the parameter "multiplier" is 2, so we can substitute the parameter for the constant:

Dollar
```
void times(int multiplier) {
   amount= amount * multiplier;
}
```

To demonstrate our thorough knowledge of Java syntax, we will want to use the *= operator (which does, it must be said, reduce duplication):

Dollar
```
void times(int multiplier) {
   amount *= multiplier;
}
```

$5 + 10 CHF = $10 if rate is 2:1
~~$5 * 2 = $10~~
Make "amount" private
Dollar side effects?
Money rounding?

We can now mark off the first test as done. Next we'll take care of those strange side effects. But first let's review. We've done the following:

- Made a list of the tests we knew we needed to have working
- Told a story with a snippet of code about how we wanted to view one operation
- Ignored the details of JUnit for the moment
- Made the test compile with stubs
- Made the test run by committing horrible sins
- Gradually generalized the working code, replacing constants with variables
- Added items to our to-do list rather than addressing them all at once

Chapter 2

Degenerate Objects

The general TDD cycle goes as follows.

1. Write a test. Think about how you would like the operation in your mind to appear in your code. You are writing a story. Invent the interface you wish you had. Include all of the elements in the story that you imagine will be necessary to calculate the right answers.

2. Make it run. Quickly getting that bar to go to green dominates everything else. If a clean, simple solution is obvious, then type it in. If the clean, simple solution is obvious but it will take you a minute, then make a note of it and get back to the main problem, which is getting the bar green in seconds. This shift in aesthetics is hard for some experienced software engineers. They only know how to follow the rules of good engineering. Quick green excuses all sins. But only for a moment.

3. Make it right. Now that the system is behaving, put the sinful ways of the recent past behind you. Step back onto the straight and narrow path of software righteousness. Remove the duplication that you have introduced, and get to green quickly.

The goal is clean code that works (thanks to Ron Jeffries for this pithy summary). Clean code that works is out of the reach of even the best programmers some of the time, and out of the reach of most programmers (like me) most of the time. Divide and conquer, baby. First we'll solve the "that works" part of the problem. Then we'll solve the "clean code" part. This is the opposite of architecture-driven development, where you solve "clean code" first, then scramble around trying to integrate into the design the things you learn as you solve the "that works" problem.

> $5 + 10 CHF = $10 if rate is 2:1
> ~~$5 * 2 = $10~~
> Make "amount" private
> **Dollar side effects?**
> Money rounding?

We got one test to work but in the process noticed something strange: when we perform an operation on a Dollar, the Dollar changes. I want to be able to write:

```
public void testMultiplication() {
    Dollar five= new Dollar(5);
    five.times(2);
    assertEquals(10, five.amount);
    five.times(3);
    assertEquals(15, five.amount);
}
```

I can't imagine a clean way to get this test to work. After the first call to times(), five isn't five any more, it's really ten. If, however, we return a new object from times(), then we can multiply our original five bucks all day and never have it change. We are changing the interface of Dollar when we make this change, so we have to change the test. That's okay. Our guesses about the right interface are no more likely to be perfect than our guesses about the right implementation.

```
public void testMultiplication() {
    Dollar five= new Dollar(5);
    Dollar product= five.times(2);
    assertEquals(10, product.amount);
    product= five.times(3);
    assertEquals(15, product.amount);
}
```

The new test won't compile until we change the declaration of Dollar.times():

Dollar
```
Dollar times(int multiplier) {
    amount *= multiplier;
    return null;
}
```

Now the test compiles, but it doesn't run. Progress! Making it run requires that we return a new `Dollar` with the correct amount:

Dollar
```
Dollar times(int multiplier) {
    return new Dollar(amount * multiplier);
}
```

> $5 + 10 CHF = $10 if rate is 2:1
> ~~$5 * 2 = $10~~
> Make "amount" private
> ~~Dollar side effects?~~
> Money rounding?

In Chapter 1, when we made a test work we started with a bogus implementation and gradually made it real. Here, we typed in what we thought was the right implementation and prayed while the tests ran (short prayers, to be sure, because running the test takes a few milliseconds). Because we got lucky and the test ran, we can cross off another item.

Following are two of the three strategies I know for quickly getting to green:

- Fake It—Return a constant and gradually replace constants with variables until you have the real code.

- Use Obvious Implementation—Type in the real implementation.

When I use TDD in practice, I commonly shift between these two modes of implementation. When everything is going smoothly and I know what to type, I put in Obvious Implementation after Obvious Implementation (running the tests each time to ensure that what's obvious to me is still obvious to the computer). As soon as I get an unexpected red bar, I back up, shift to faking implementations, and refactor to the right code. When my confidence returns, I go back to Obvious Implementations.

There is a third style of TDD, Triangulation, which we will demonstrate in Chapter 3. However, to review, we

- Translated a design objection (side effects) into a test case that failed because of the objection

- Got the code to compile quickly with a stub implementation

- Made the test work by typing in what seemed to be the right code

The translation of a feeling (for example, disgust at side effects) into a test (for example, multiply the same Dollar twice) is a common theme of TDD. The longer I do this, the better able I am to translate my aesthetic judgments into tests. When I can do this, my design discussions become much more interesting. First we can talk about whether the system should work like *this* or like *that*. Once we decide on the correct behavior, we can talk about the best way of achieving that behavior. We can speculate about truth and beauty all we want over beers, but while we are programming we can leave airy-fairy discussions behind and talk cases.

Chapter 3

Equality for All

If I have an integer and I add 1 to it, I don't expect the original integer to change, I expect to use the new value. Objects usually don't behave that way. If I have a contract and I add one to its coverage, then the contract's coverage should change (yes, yes, subject to all sorts of interesting business rules which do *not* concern us here).

We can use objects as values, as we are using our Dollar now. The pattern for this is Value Object. One of the constraints on Value Objects is that the values of the instance variables of the object never change once they have been set in the constructor.

There is one huge advantage to using Value Objects: you don't have to worry about aliasing problems. Say I have one check and I set its amount to $5, and then I set another check's amount to the same $5. Some of the nastiest bugs in my career have come when changing the first check's value inadvertently changed the second check's value. This is aliasing.

When you have Value Objects, you needn't worry about aliasing. If I have $5, then I am guaranteed that it will always and forever be $5. If someone wants $7, then they will have to make an entirely new object.

> $5 + 10 CHF = $10 if rate is 2:1
> ~~$5 * 2 = $10~~
> Make "amount" private
> ~~Dollar side effects?~~
> Money rounding?
> equals()

One implication of Value Objects is that all operations must return a new object, as we saw in Chapter 2. Another implication is that Value Objects should implement equals(), because one $5 is pretty much as good as another.

15

> $5 + 10 CHF = $10 if rate is 2:1
> ~~$5 * 2 = $10~~
> Make "amount" private
> ~~Dollar side effects?~~
> Money rounding?
> **equals()**
> hashCode()

If you use Dollars as the key to a hash table, then you have to implement hashCode() if you implement equals(). We'll put that on the to-do list, too, and get to it when it's a problem.

You aren't thinking about the implementation of equals(), are you? Good. Me neither. After snapping the back of my hand with a ruler, I'm thinking about how to test equality. First, $5 should equal $5:

```
public void testEquality() {
    assertTrue(new Dollar(5).equals(new Dollar(5)));
}
```

The bar turns obligingly red. The fake implementation is just to return true:

Dollar
```
public boolean equals(Object object) {
    return true;
}
```

You and I both know that true is really "5 == 5", which is really "amount == 5", which is really "amount == dollar.amount". If I went through these steps, though, I wouldn't be able to demonstrate the third and most conservative implementation strategy: Triangulation.

If two receiving stations at a known distance from each other can both measure the direction of a radio signal, then there is enough information to calculate the range and bearing of the signal (if you remember more trigonometry than I do, anyway). This calculation is called Triangulation.

By analogy, when we triangulate, we only generalize code when we have two examples or more. We briefly ignore the duplication between test and model code. When the second example demands a more general solution, then and only then do we generalize.

So, to triangulate we need a second example. How about $5 != $6?

```
public void testEquality() {
    assertTrue(new Dollar(5).equals(new Dollar(5)));
    assertFalse(new Dollar(5).equals(new Dollar(6)));
}
```

Now we need to generalize equality:

Dollar
```
public boolean equals(Object object) {
   Dollar dollar= (Dollar) object;
   return amount == dollar.amount;
}
```

> $5 + 10 CHF = $10 if rate is 2:1
> ~~$5 * 2 = $10~~
> Make "amount" private
> ~~Dollar side effects?~~
> Money rounding?
> ~~equals()~~
> hashCode()

We could have used Triangulation to drive the generalization of times() also. If we had $5 x 2 = $10 and $5 x 3 = $15, then we would no longer have been able to return a constant.

Triangulation feels funny to me. I use it only when I am completely unsure of how to refactor. If I can see how to eliminate duplication between code and tests and create the general solution, then I just do it. Why would I need to write another test to give me permission to write what I probably could have written in the first place?

However, when the design thoughts just aren't coming, Triangulation provides a chance to think about the problem from a slightly different direction. What axes of variability are you trying to support in your design? Make some of them vary, and the answer may become clearer.

> $5 + 10 CHF = $10 if rate is 2:1
> ~~$5 * 2 = $10~~
> Make "amount" private
> ~~Dollar side effects?~~
> Money rounding?
> ~~equals()~~
> hashCode()
> Equal null
> Equal object

So, equality is done for the moment. But what about comparing with null and comparing with other objects? These are commonly used operations but not necessary at the moment, so we'll add them to the to-do list.

Now that we have equality, we can directly compare Dollars to Dollars. That will let us make "amount" private, as all good instance variables should be. To review the above, we

- Noticed that our design pattern (Value Object) implied an operation
- Tested for that operation
- Implemented it simply
- Didn't refactor immediately, but instead tested further
- Refactored to capture the two cases at once

Chapter 4

Privacy

$5 + 10 CHF = $10 if rate is 2:1

~~$5 * 2 = $10~~

Make "amount" private

~~Dollar side effects?~~

Money rounding?

~~equals()~~

hashCode()

Equal null

Equal object

Now that we have defined equality, we can use it to make our tests more "speaking." Conceptually, the operation Dollar.times() should return a Dollar whose value is the value of the receiver times the multiplier. Our test doesn't exactly say that:

```
public void testMultiplication() {
   Dollar five= new Dollar(5);
   Dollar product= five.times(2);
   assertEquals(10, product.amount);
   product= five.times(3);
   assertEquals(15, product.amount);
}
```

We can rewrite the first assertion to compare Dollars to Dollars:

```
public void testMultiplication() {
   Dollar five= new Dollar(5);
   Dollar product= five.times(2);
   assertEquals(new Dollar(10), product);
   product= five.times(3);
   assertEquals(15, product.amount);
}
```

That looks better, so we rewrite the second assertion, too:

```
public void testMultiplication() {
    Dollar five= new Dollar(5);
    Dollar product= five.times(2);
    assertEquals(new Dollar(10), product);
    product= five.times(3);
    assertEquals(new Dollar(15), product);
}
```

Now the temporary variable product isn't helping much, so we can inline it:

```
public void testMultiplication() {
    Dollar five= new Dollar(5);
    assertEquals(new Dollar(10), five.times(2));
    assertEquals(new Dollar(15), five.times(3));
}
```

This test speaks to us more clearly, as if it were an assertion of truth, not a sequence of operations.

With these changes to the test, Dollar is now the only class using its amount instance variable, so we can make it private:

Dollar
```
private int amount;
```

> $5 + 10 CHF = $10 if rate is 2:1
> ~~$5 * 2 = $10~~
> ~~Make "amount" private~~
> ~~Dollar side effects?~~
> Money rounding?
> ~~equals()~~
> hashCode()
> Equal null
> Equal object

And we can cross another item off the to-do list. Notice that we have opened ourselves up to a risk. If the test for equality fails to accurately check that equality is working, then the test for multiplication could also fail to accurately check that multiplication is working. This is a risk that we actively manage in TDD. We aren't striving for perfection. By saying everything two ways—both as code and as tests—we hope to reduce our defects enough to move forward with confidence. From time to time our reasoning will fail us and a defect will slip through. When that happens, we learn our lesson about the test we should have written and move on. The rest of the time we go forward boldly under our bravely flapping green bar (my bar doesn't actually flap, but one can dream.)

To review, we

- Used functionality just developed to improve a test

- Noticed that if two tests fail at once we're sunk

- Proceeded in spite of the risk

- Used new functionality in the object under test to reduce coupling between the tests and the code

Chapter 5

Franc-ly Speaking

> $5 + 10 CHF = $10 if rate is 2:1
> ~~$5 * 2 = $10~~
> ~~Make "amount" private~~
> ~~Dollar side effects?~~
> Money rounding?
> ~~equals()~~
> hashCode()
> Equal null
> Equal object
> **5 CHF * 2 = 10 CHF**

How are we going to approach the first test, the most interesting test, on that list? It still seems to be a big leap. I'm not sure I can write a test that I can implement in one little step. A prerequisite seems to be having an object like Dollar, but to represent francs. If we can get the object Franc to work the way that the object Dollar works now, we'll be closer to being able to write and run the mixed addition test.

We can copy and edit the Dollar test:

```
public void testFrancMultiplication() {
    Franc five= new Franc(5);
    assertEquals(new Franc(10), five.times(2));
    assertEquals(new Franc(15), five.times(3));
}
```

(Aren't you glad we simplified the test in Chapter 4? That has made our job here easier. Isn't it amazing how often things work out like this in books? I didn't actually plan it that way this time, but I won't make promises for the future.)

What short step will get us to a green bar? Copying the Dollar code and replacing Dollar with Franc.

Stop. Hold on. I can hear the aesthetically inclined among you sneering and spitting. Copy-and-paste reuse? The death of abstraction? The killer of clean design?

If you're upset, take a cleansing breath. In through the nose . . . hold it 1, 2, 3 . . . out through the mouth. There. Remember, our cycle has different phases (they go by quickly, often in seconds, but they are phases.):

1. Write a test.

2. Make it compile.

3. Run it to see that it fails.

4. Make it run.

5. Remove duplication.

The different phases have different purposes. They call for different styles of solution, different aesthetic viewpoints. The first three phases need to go by quickly, so we get to a known state with the new functionality. We can commit any number of sins to get there, because speed trumps design, just for that brief moment.

Now I'm worried. I've given you a license to abandon all the principles of good design. Off you go to your teams—"Kent says all that design stuff doesn't matter." Halt. The cycle is not complete. A four-legged Aeron chair falls over. The first four steps of the cycle won't work without the fifth. Good design at good times. Make it run, make it right.

There, I feel better. Now I'm sure you won't show anyone except your partner your code until you've removed the duplication. Where were we? Ah, yes. Violating all the tenets of good design in the interest of speed (penance for our sin will occupy the next several chapters).

Franc

```java
class Franc {
    private int amount;

    Franc(int amount) {
        this.amount= amount;
    }

    Franc times(int multiplier) {
        return new Franc(amount * multiplier);
    }

    public boolean equals(Object object) {
        Franc franc= (Franc) object;
        return amount == franc.amount;
    }
}
```

$5 + 10 CHF = $10 if rate is 2:1
~~$5 * 2 = $10~~
~~Make "amount" private~~
~~Dollar side effects?~~
Money rounding?
~~equals()~~
hashCode()
Equal null
Equal object
~~5 CHF * 2 = 10 CHF~~
Dollar/Franc duplication
Common equals
Common times

Because the step to running code was so short, we were even able to skip the "make it compile" step.

Now we have duplication galore, and we have to eliminate it before writing our next test. We'll start by generalizing equals(). However, we can cross an item off our to-do list, even though we have to add two more. Reviewing, we

- Couldn't tackle a big test, so we invented a small test that represented progress

- Wrote the test by shamelessly duplicating and editing

- Even worse, made the test work by copying and editing model code wholesale

- Promised ourselves we wouldn't go home until the duplication was gone

Chapter 6

Equality for All, Redux

$5 + 10 CHF = $10 if rate is 2:1
~~$5 * 2 = $10~~
~~Make "amount" private~~
~~Dollar side effects?~~
Money rounding?
~~equals()~~
hashCode()
Equal null
Equal object
~~5 CHF * 2 = 10 CHF~~
Dollar/Franc duplication
Common equals
Common times

There is a fabulous sequence in *Crossing to Safety* in which author Wallace Stegner describes a character's workshop. Every item is perfectly in place, the floor is spotless, all is order and cleanliness. The character, however, has never made anything. "Preparing has been his life's work. He prepares, then he cleans up." (This is also the book whose ending sent me audibly blubbering in business class on a trans-Atlantic 747. Read with caution.)

We avoided this trap in Chapter 5. We actually got a new test case working. But we sinned mightily in copying and pasting tons of code in order to do it quickly. Now it is time to clean up.

One possibility is to make one of our classes extend the other. I tried it, and it hardly saves any code at all. Instead, we are going to find a common superclass for the two classes, as shown in Figure 6.1. (I tried this already, too, and it works out great, although it will take a while.)

Figure 6.1 *A common superclass for two classes*

What if we had a Money class to capture the common equals code? We can start small:

Money
```
class Money
```

All of the tests still run—not that we could possibly have broken anything, but it's a good time to run the tests anyway. If Dollar extends Money, that can't possibly break anything.

Dollar
```
class Dollar extends Money {
    private int amount;
}
```

Can it? No, the tests still all run. Now we can move the amount instance variable up to Money:

Money
```
class Money {
    protected int amount;
}
```

Dollar
```
class Dollar extends Money {
}
```

The visibility has to change from private to protected so that the subclass can still see it. (Had we wanted to go even slower, we could have declared the field in Money in one step and then removed it from Dollar in a second step. I'm feeling bold.)

Now we can work on getting the equals() code ready to move up. First we change the declaration of the temporary variable:

Dollar
```
public boolean equals(Object object) {
    Money dollar= (Dollar) object;
    return amount == dollar.amount;
}
```

All the tests still run. Now we change the cast:

Dollar
```
public boolean equals(Object object) {
   Money dollar= (Money) object;
   return amount == dollar.amount;
}
```

To be communicative, we should also change the name of the temporary variable:

Dollar
```
public boolean equals(Object object) {
   Money money= (Money) object;
   return amount == money.amount;
}
```

Now we can move it from Dollar to Money:

Money
```
public boolean equals(Object object) {
   Money money= (Money) object;
   return amount == money.amount;
}
```

Now we need to eliminate Franc.equals(). First we notice that the tests for equality don't cover comparing Francs to Francs. Our sins in copying code are catching up with us. Before we change the code, we'll write the tests that should have been there in the first place.

You will often be implementing TDD in code that doesn't have adequate tests (at least for the next decade or so). When you don't have enough tests, you are bound to come across refactorings that aren't supported by tests. You could make a refactoring mistake and the tests would all still run. What do you do?

Write the tests you wish you had. If you don't, you will eventually break something while refactoring. Then you'll get bad feelings about refactoring and stop doing it so much. Then your design will deteriorate. You'll be fired. Your dog will leave you. You will stop paying attention to your nutrition. Your teeth will go bad. So, to keep your teeth healthy, retroactively test before refactoring.

Fortunately, here the tests are easy to write. We just copy the tests for Dollar:

```
public void testEquality() {

   assertTrue(new Dollar(5).equals(new Dollar(5)));
   assertFalse(new Dollar(5).equals(new Dollar(6)));
   assertTrue(new Franc(5).equals(new Franc(5)));
   assertFalse(new Franc(5).equals(new Franc(6)));
}
```

More duplication, two lines more! We'll atone for these sins, too.

Tests in place, we can have Franc extend Money:

Franc
```
class Franc extends Money {
   private int amount;
}
```

We can delete Franc's field amount in favor of the one in Money:

Franc
```
class Franc extends Money {
}
```

Franc.equals() is almost the same as Money.equals(). If we make them precisely the same, then we can delete the implementation in Franc without changing the meaning of the program. First we change the declaration of the temporary variable:

Franc
```
public boolean equals(Object object) {
   Money franc= (Franc) object;
   return amount == franc.amount;
}
```

Then we change the cast:

Franc
```
public boolean equals(Object object) {
   Money franc= (Money) object;
   return amount == franc.amount;
}
```

Do we really have to change the name of the temporary variable to match the superclass? I'll leave it up to your conscience.... Okay, we'll do it:

Franc
```
public boolean equals(Object object) {
   Money money= (Money) object;
   return amount == money.amount;
}
```

$5 + 10 CHF = $10 if rate is 2:1
~~$5 * 2 = $10~~
~~Make "amount" private~~
~~Dollar side effects?~~
Money rounding?
~~equals()~~

hashCode()
Equal null
Equal object
~~5 CHF * 2 = 10 CHF~~
Dollar/Franc duplication
~~Common equals~~
Common times
Compare Francs with Dollars

Now there is no difference between Franc.equals() and Money.equals(), so we delete the redundant implementation in Franc. And run the tests. They run.

What happens when we compare Francs with Dollars? We'll get to that in Chapter 7. Reviewing what we did here, we

- Stepwise moved common code from one class (Dollar) to a superclass (Money)

- Made a second class (Franc) a subclass also

- Reconciled two implementations—equals()—before eliminating the redundant one

Chapter 7

Apples and Oranges

$5 + 10 CHF = $10 if rate is 2:1
~~$5 * 2 = $10~~
~~Make "amount" private~~
~~Dollar side effects?~~
Money rounding?
~~equals()~~
hashCode()
Equal null
Equal object
~~5 CHF * 2 = 10 CHF~~
Dollar/Franc duplication
~~Common equals~~
Common times
Compare Francs with Dollars

The thought struck us at the end of Chapter 6: what happens when we compare Francs with Dollars? We dutifully turned our dreadful thought into an item on our to-do list. But we just can't get it out of our heads. What does happen?

```
public void testEquality() {
    assertTrue(new Dollar(5).equals(new Dollar(5)));
    assertFalse(new Dollar(5).equals(new Dollar(6)));
    assertTrue(new Franc(5).equals(new Franc(5)));
    assertFalse(new Franc(5).equals(new Franc(6)));
    assertFalse(new Franc(5).equals(new Dollar(5)));
}
```

It fails. Dollars are Francs. Before you Swiss shoppers get all excited, let's try to fix the code. The equality code needs to check that it isn't comparing Dollars with Francs. We can do this right now by comparing the class of the two objects—two Moneys are equal only if their amounts and classes are equal.

Money
```
public boolean equals(Object object) {
    Money money = (Money) object;
    return amount == money.amount
        && getClass().equals(money.getClass());
}
```

Using classes this way in model code is a bit smelly. We would like to use a criterion that makes sense in the domain of finance, not in the domain of Java objects. But we don't currently have anything like a currency, and this doesn't seem to be sufficient reason to introduce one, so this will have to do for the moment.

$5 + 10 CHF = $10 if rate is 2:1
~~$5 * 2 = $10~~
~~Make "amount" private~~
~~Dollar side effects?~~
Money rounding?
~~equals()~~
hashCode()
Equal null
Equal object
~~5 CHF * 2 = 10 CHF~~
Dollar/Franc duplication
~~Common equals~~
Common times
~~Compare Francs to Dollars~~
Currency?

Now we really need to get rid of the common times() code, so we can get to mixed currency arithmetic. Before we do, however, we can review our grand accomplishments for this chapter. We

- Took an objection that was bothering us and turned it into a test

- Made the test run a reasonable, but not perfect way—getClass()

- Decided not to introduce more design until we had a better motivation

Chapter 8

Makin' Objects

$5 + 10 CHF = $10 if rate is 2:1
~~$5 * 2 = $10~~
~~Make "amount" private~~
~~Dollar side effects?~~
Money rounding?
~~equals()~~
hashCode()
Equal null
Equal object
~~5 CHF * 2 = 10 CHF~~
Dollar/Franc duplication
~~Common equals~~
Common times
~~Compare Francs to Dollars~~
Currency?

The two implementations of times() are remarkably similar:

Franc
```
Franc times(int multiplier) {
    return new Franc(amount * multiplier);
}
```

Dollar
```
Dollar times(int multiplier) {
    return new Dollar(amount * multiplier);
}
```

We can take a step toward reconciling them by making them both return a Money:

Franc
```
Money times(int multiplier) {
    return new Franc(amount * multiplier);
}
```

Dollar
```
Money times(int multiplier) {
    return new Dollar(amount * multiplier);
}
```

The next step forward is not obvious. The two subclasses of Money aren't doing enough work to justify their existence, so we would like to eliminate them. But we can't do it with one big step, because that wouldn't make a very effective demonstration of TDD.

Okay, we would be one step closer to eliminating the subclasses if there were fewer references to the subclasses directly. We can introduce a factory method in Money that returns a Dollar. We would use it like this:

```
public void testMultiplication() {
    Dollar five = Money.dollar(5);
    assertEquals(new Dollar(10), five.times(2));
    assertEquals(new Dollar(15), five.times(3));
}
```

The implementation creates and returns a Dollar:

Money
```
static Dollar dollar(int amount) {
    return new Dollar(amount);
}
```

But we want references to Dollars to disappear, so we need to change the declaration in the test:

```
public void testMultiplication() {
    Money five = Money.dollar(5);
    assertEquals(new Dollar(10), five.times(2));
    assertEquals(new Dollar(15), five.times(3));
}
```

Our compiler politely informs us that times() is not defined for Money. We aren't ready to implement it just yet, so we make Money abstract (I suppose we should have done that to begin with?) and declare Money.times():

Money
```
abstract class Money
abstract Money times(int multiplier);
```

Now we can change the declaration of the factory method:

Money
```
static Money dollar(int amount) {
    return new Dollar(amount);
}
```

The tests all run, so at least we haven't broken anything. We can now use our factory method everywhere in the tests:

```java
public void testMultiplication() {
    Money five = Money.dollar(5);
    assertEquals(Money.dollar(10), five.times(2));
    assertEquals(Money.dollar(15), five.times(3));
}
public void testEquality() {
    assertTrue(Money.dollar(5).equals(Money.dollar(5)));
    assertFalse(Money.dollar(5).equals(Money.dollar(6)));
    assertTrue(new Franc(5).equals(new Franc(5)));
    assertFalse(new Franc(5).equals(new Franc(6)));
    assertFalse(new Franc(5).equals(Money.dollar(5)));
}
```

We are now in a slightly better position than before. No client code knows that there is a subclass called Dollar. By decoupling the tests from the existence of the subclasses, we have given ourselves freedom to change inheritance without affecting any model code.

Before we go blindly changing the testFrancMultiplication, we notice that it isn't testing any logic that isn't tested by the test for Dollar multiplication. If we delete the test, will we lose any confidence in the code? Still a little, so we leave it there. But it's suspicious.

```java
public void testEquality() {
    assertTrue(Money.dollar(5).equals(Money.dollar(5)));
    assertFalse(Money.dollar(5).equals(Money.dollar(6)));
    assertTrue(Money.franc(5).equals(Money.franc(5)));
    assertFalse(Money.franc(5).equals(Money.franc(6)));
    assertFalse(Money.franc(5).equals(Money.dollar(5)));
}

public void testFrancMultiplication() {
    Money five = Money.franc(5);
    assertEquals(Money.franc(10), five.times(2));
    assertEquals(Money.franc(15), five.times(3));
}
```

The implementation is just like Money.dollar():

Money
```java
static Money franc(int amount) {
    return new Franc(amount);
}
```

$5 + 10 CHF = $10 if rate is 2:1
~~$5 * 2 = $10~~
~~Make "amount" private~~
~~Dollar side effects?~~
Money rounding?
~~equals()~~
hashCode()
Equal null
Equal object
~~5 CHF * 2 = 10 CHF~~
Dollar/Franc duplication
~~Common equals~~
Common times
~~Compare Francs to Dollars~~
Currency?
Delete testFrancMultiplication?

Next we'll get rid of the duplication of times(). For now, to review, we

- Took a step toward eliminating duplication by reconciling the signatures of two variants of the same method—times()

- Moved at least a declaration of the method to the common superclass

- Decoupled test code from the existence of concrete subclasses by introducing factory methods

- Noticed that when the subclasses disappear some tests will be redundant, but took no action

Chapter 9

Times We're Livin' In

$5 + 10 CHF = $10 if rate is 2:1
~~$5 * 2 = $10~~
~~Make "amount" private~~
~~Dollar side effects?~~
Money rounding?
~~equals()~~
hashCode()
Equal null
Equal object
~~5 CHF * 2 = 10 CHF~~
Dollar/Franc duplication
~~Common equals~~
Common times
~~Compare Francs to Dollars~~
Currency?
Delete testFrancMultiplication?

What is there on our to-do list that might help us to eliminate those pesky useless subclasses? What would happen if we introduced the notion of currency?

How do we want to implement currencies at the moment? I blew it, again. Before the ruler comes out, I'll rephrase: How do we want to test for currencies at the moment? There. Knuckles saved, for the moment.

We may want to have complicated objects representing currencies, with flyweight factories to ensure we create no more objects than we really need. But for the moment, strings will do:

```java
public void testCurrency() {
    assertEquals("USD", Money.dollar(1).currency());
    assertEquals("CHF", Money.franc(1).currency());
}
```

First we declare currency() in Money:

Money
```
abstract String currency();
```

Then we implement it in both subclasses:

Franc
```
String currency() {
    return "CHF";
}
```

Dollar
```
String currency() {
    return "USD";
}
```

We want the same implementation to suffice for both classes. We could store the currency in an instance variable and just return the variable. (I'll start going a little faster with the refactorings in the interest of time. If I go too fast, please tell me to slow down. Oh wait, this is a book—perhaps I just won't speed up much.)

Franc
```
private String currency;
Franc(int amount) {
    this.amount = amount;
    currency = "CHF";
}
String currency() {
    return currency;
}
```

We can do the same with Dollar:

Dollar
```
private String currency;
Dollar(int amount) {
    this.amount = amount;
    currency = "USD";
}
String currency() {
    return currency;
}
```

Now we can push up the declaration of the variable and the implementation of currency(), because they are identical:

Money
```
protected String currency;
String currency() {
   return currency;
}
```

If we move the constant strings "USD" and "CHF" to the static factory methods, then the two constructors will be identical and we can create a common implementation.

First we'll add a parameter to the constructor:

Franc
```
Franc(int amount, String currency) {
   this.amount = amount;
   this.currency = "CHF";
}
```

This breaks the two callers of the constructor:

Money
```
static Money franc(int amount) {
   return new Franc(amount, null);
}
```

Franc
```
Money times(int multiplier) {
   return new Franc(amount * multiplier, null);
}
```

Wait a minute! Why is Franc.times() calling the constructor instead of the factory method? Do we want to make this change now, or will we wait? The dogmatic answer is that we'll wait, not interrupting what we're doing. The answer in my practice is that I will entertain a brief interruption, but only a brief one, and I will never interrupt an interruption (Jim Coplien taught me this rule). To be realistic, we'll clean up times() before proceeding:

Franc
```
Money times(int multiplier) {
   return Money.franc(amount * multiplier);
}
```

Now the factory method can pass "CHF":

Money
```
static Money franc(int amount) {
   return new Franc(amount, "CHF");
}
```

And finally we can assign the parameter to the instance variable:

Franc
```
Franc(int amount, String currency) {
    this.amount = amount;
    this.currency = currency;
}
```

I'm feeling defensive again about taking such teeny-tiny steps. Am I recommending that you actually work this way? No. I'm recommending that you be able to work this way. What I did just now was to work in larger steps and make a stupid mistake halfway through. I unwound a minute's-worth of changes, shifted to a lower gear, and did it over with little steps. I'm feeling better now, so we'll see if we can make the analogous change to Dollar in one swell foop:

Money
```
static Money dollar(int amount) {
    return new Dollar(amount, "USD");
}
```

Dollar
```
Dollar(int amount, String currency) {
    this.amount = amount;
    this.currency = currency;
}
Money times(int multiplier) {
    return Money.dollar(amount * multiplier);
}
```

And it worked first time. Whew!

This is the kind of tuning you will be doing constantly with TDD. Are the teeny-tiny steps feeling restrictive? Take bigger steps. Are you feeling a little unsure? Take smaller steps. TDD is a steering process—a little this way, a little that way. There is no right step size, now and forever.

The two constructors are now identical, so we can push up the implementation:

Money
```
Money(int amount, String currency) {
    this.amount = amount;
    this.currency = currency;
}
```

Franc
```
Franc(int amount, String currency) {
    super(amount, currency);
}
```

Dollar

```
Dollar(int amount, String currency) {
   super(amount, currency);
}
```

$5 + 10 CHF = $10 if rate is 2:1
~~$5 * 2 = $10~~
~~Make "amount" private~~
~~Dollar side effects?~~
Money rounding?
~~equals()~~
hashCode()
Equal null
Equal object
~~5 CHF * 2 = 10 CHF~~
Dollar/Franc duplication
~~Common equals~~
Common times
~~Compare Francs to Dollars~~
~~Currency?~~
Delete testFrancMultiplication?

We're almost ready to push up the implementation of times() and eliminate the subclasses, but first, to review, we

- Were a little stuck on big design ideas, so we worked on something small we noticed earlier

- Reconciled the two constructors by moving the variation to the caller (the factory method)

- Interrupted a refactoring for a little twist, using the factory method in times()

- Repeated an analogous refactoring (doing to Dollar what we just did to Franc) in one big step

- Pushed up the identical constructors

Chapter 10

Interesting Times

$5 + 10 CHF = $10 if rate is 2:1
~~$5 * 2 = $10~~
~~Make "amount" private~~
~~Dollar side effects?~~
Money rounding?
~~equals()~~
hashCode()
Equal null
Equal object
~~5 CHF * 2 = 10 CHF~~
Dollar/Franc duplication
~~Common equals~~
Common times
~~Compare Francs to Dollars~~
~~Currency?~~
Delete testFrancMultiplication?

When we are done with this chapter, we will have a single class to represent Money. The two implementations of times() are close, but not identical:

Franc
```
Money times(int multiplier) {
    return Money.franc(amount * multiplier);
}
```

Dollar
```
Money times(int multiplier) {
    return Money.dollar(amount * multiplier);
}
```

There's no obvious way to make them identical. Sometimes you have to go backward to go forward, a little like solving a Rubik's Cube. What happens if we inline the factory methods? (I know, I know, we just called the factory method for the first time just one chapter ago. Frustrating, isn't it?)

Franc
```
Money times(int multiplier) {
    return new Franc(amount * multiplier, "CHF");
}
```

Dollar
```
Money times(int multiplier) {
    return new Dollar(amount * multiplier, "USD");
}
```

In Franc, however, we know that the currency instance variable is always "CHF", so we can write:

Franc
```
Money times(int multiplier) {
    return new Franc(amount * multiplier, currency);
}
```

That works. The same trick works in Dollar:

Dollar
```
Money times(int multiplier) {
    return new Dollar(amount * multiplier, currency);
}
```

We're almost there. Does it really matter whether we have a Franc or a Money? We could carefully reason about this given our knowledge of the system, but we have clean code and we have tests that give us confidence that the clean code works. Rather than apply minutes of suspect reasoning, we can just ask the computer by making the change and running the tests. In teaching TDD, I see this situation all the time—excellent software engineers spending 5 to 10 minutes reasoning about a question that the computer could answer in 15 seconds. Without the tests you have no choice, you have to reason. With the tests you can decide whether an experiment would answer the question faster. Sometimes you should just ask the computer.

To run our experiment, we change Franc.times() to return a Money:

Franc
```
Money times(int multiplier) {
    return new Money(amount * multiplier, currency);
}
```

The compiler tells us that Money must be a concrete class:

Money
```
class Money
Money times(int amount) {
    return null;
}
```

And we get a red bar. The error message says, "expected:<Money.Franc@31aebf> but was: <Money.Money@478a43>". Not as helpful as we perhaps would like. We can define toString() to give us a better error message:

Money
```
public String toString() {
    return amount + " " + currency;
}
```

Whoa! Code without a test? Can you do that? We could certainly have written a test for toString() before we coded it. However,

- We are about to see the results on the screen.

- Because toString() is used only for debug output, the risk of it failing is low.

- We already have a red bar, and we'd prefer not to write a test when we have a red bar.

Exception noted.

Now the error message says: "expected:<10 CHF> but was:<10 CHF>". That's a little better, but still confusing. We have the right data in the answer, but the class is wrong—Money instead of Franc. The problem is in our implementation of equals():

Money
```
public boolean equals(Object object) {
    Money money = (Money) object;
    return amount == money.amount
        && getClass().equals(money.getClass());
}
```

We really should be checking to see that the currencies are the same, not that the classes are the same.

We'd prefer not to write a test when we have a red bar. But we are about to change real model code, and we can't change model code without a test. The conservative course is to back out the change that caused the red bar so we're back to green. Then we can change the test for equals(), fix the implementation, and retry the original change.

This time, we'll be conservative. (Sometimes I plough ahead and write a test on a red, but not while the children are awake.)

Franc
```
Money times(int multiplier) {
    return new Franc(amount * multiplier, currency);
}
```

That gets us back to green. The situation that we had was a Franc(10, "CHF") and a Money(10, "CHF") that were reported to be not equal, even though we would like them to be equal. We can use exactly this for our test:

```
public void testDifferentClassEquality() {
    assertTrue(new Money(10, "CHF").equals(new Franc(10, "CHF")));
}
```

It fails, as expected. The equals() code should compare currencies, not classes:

Money
```
public boolean equals(Object object) {
    Money money = (Money) object;
    return amount == money.amount
        && currency().equals(money.currency());
}
```

Now we can return a Money from Franc.times() and still pass the tests:

Franc
```
Money times(int multiplier) {
    return new Money(amount * multiplier, currency);
}
```

Will the same work for Dollar.times()?

Dollar
```
Money times(int multiplier) {
    return new Money(amount * multiplier, currency);
}
```

Yes! Now the two implementations are identical, so we can push them up.

Money
```
Money times(int multiplier) {
    return new Money(amount * multiplier, currency);
}
```

$5 + 10 CHF = $10 if rate is 2:1
$5 * 2 = $10
Make "amount" private
Dollar side effects?
Money rounding?
equals()
hashCode()
Equal null
Equal object
5 CHF * 2 = 10 CHF

Dollar/Franc duplication
~~Common equals~~
~~Common times~~
~~Compare Francs to Dollars~~
~~Currency?~~
Delete testFrancMultiplication?

Multiplication in place, we are ready to eliminate the stupid subclasses. To review, we:

- Reconciled two methods—times()—by first inlining the methods they called and then replacing constants with variables

- Wrote a toString() without a test just to help us debug

- Tried a change (returning Money instead of Franc) and let the tests tell us whether it worked

- Backed out an experiment and wrote another test. Making the test work made the experiment work

Chapter 11

The Root of All Evil

$5 + 10 CHF = $10 if rate is 2:1
~~$5 * 2 = $10~~
~~Make "amount" private~~
~~Dollar side effects?~~
Money rounding?
~~equals()~~
hashCode()
Equal null
Equal object
~~5 CHF * 2 = 10 CHF~~
Dollar/Franc duplication
~~Common equals~~
~~Common times~~
~~Compare Francs to Dollars~~
~~Currency?~~
Delete testFrancMultiplication?

The two subclasses, Dollar and Franc, have only their constructors. But because a constructor is not reason enough to have a subclass, we want to delete the subclasses.

We can replace references to the subclasses with references to the superclass without changing the meaning of the code. First Franc:

Franc
```
static Money franc(int amount) {
    return new Money(amount, "CHF");
}
```

Then Dollar:

Dollar
```
static Money dollar(int amount) {
    return new Money(amount, "USD");
}
```

Now there are no references to Dollar, so we can delete it. Franc, on the other hand, still has one reference, in the test we just wrote.

```
public void testDifferentClassEquality() {
    assertTrue(new Money(10, "CHF").equals(new Franc(10, "CHF")));
}
```

Is equality covered well enough elsewhere that we can delete this test? Looking at the other equality test,

```
public void testEquality() {
    assertTrue(Money.dollar(5).equals(Money.dollar(5)));
    assertFalse(Money.dollar(5).equals(Money.dollar(6)));
    assertTrue(Money.franc(5).equals(Money.franc(5)));
    assertFalse(Money.franc(5).equals(Money.franc(6)));
    assertFalse(Money.franc(5).equals(Money.dollar(5)));
}
```

it looks as though we have the cases for equality well covered—too well covered, actually. We can delete the third and fourth assertions because they duplicate the exercise of the first and second assertions:

```
public void testEquality() {
    assertTrue(Money.dollar(5).equals(Money.dollar(5)));
    assertFalse(Money.dollar(5).equals(Money.dollar(6)));
    assertFalse(Money.franc(5).equals(Money.dollar(5)));
}
```

$5 + 10 CHF = $10 if rate is 2:1
~~$5 * 2 = $10~~
~~Make "amount" private~~
~~Dollar side effects?~~
Money rounding?
~~equals()~~
hashCode()
Equal null
Equal object
~~5 CHF * 2 = 10 CHF~~
~~Dollar/Franc duplication~~
~~Common equals~~
~~Common times~~
~~Compare Francs to Dollars~~
~~Currency?~~
~~Delete testFrancMultiplication?~~

The test we wrote forcing us to compare currencies instead of classes makes sense only if there are multiple classes. Because we are trying to eliminate the

Franc class, a test to ensure that the system works if there is a Franc class is a burden, not a help. Away testDifferentClassEquality() goes, and Franc goes with it.

Similarly, there are separate tests for dollar and franc multiplication. Looking at the code, we can see that there is no difference in the logic at the moment based on the currency (there was a difference when there were two classes). We can delete testFrancMultiplication() without losing any confidence in the behavior of the system.

Single class in place, we are ready to tackle addition. First, to review, we

- Finished gutting subclasses and deleted them

- Eliminated tests that made sense with the old code structure but were redundant with the new code structure

Chapter 12

Addition, Finally

$5 + 10 CHF = $10 if rate is 2:1

It's a new day, and our to-do list has become a bit cluttered, so we'll copy the pending items to a fresh list. (I like physically copying to-do items to a new list. If there are lots of little items, I tend just to take care of them rather than copy them. Little stuff that otherwise might build up gets taken care of just because I'm lazy. Play to your strengths.)

$5 + 10 CHF = $10 if rate is 2:1
$5 + $5 = $10

I'm not sure how to write the story of the whole addition, so we'll start with a simpler example: $5 + $5 = $10.

```
public void testSimpleAddition() {
    Money sum= Money.dollar(5).plus(Money.dollar(5));
    assertEquals(Money.dollar(10), sum);
}
```

We could fake the implementation by just returning "Money.dollar(10)", but the implementation seems obvious. We'll try:

Money
```
Money plus(Money addend) {
    return new Money(amount + addend.amount, currency);
}
```

(In general, I will begin speeding up the implementations to save trees and keep your interest. Where the design isn't obvious, I will still fake the implementation and refactor. I hope you will see through this how TDD gives you control over the size of steps.)

Having said that I was going to go much faster, I will immediately go much slower—not in getting the tests working, but in writing the test itself. There are times and tests that call for careful thought. How are we going to represent multi-currency arithmetic? This is one of those times for careful thought.

The most difficult design constraint is that we want most of the code in the system to be unaware that it potentially is dealing with multiple currencies. One possible strategy is to immediately convert all money values into a reference currency. (I'll let you guess which reference currency American imperialist programmers generally choose.) However, this doesn't allow exchange rates to vary easily.

Instead we would like a solution that lets us conveniently represent multiple exchange rates, and still allows most arithmetic-like expressions to look like, well, arithmetic.

Objects to the rescue. When the object we have doesn't behave the way we want it to, we make another object with the same external protocol (an imposter) but a different implementation.

This probably sounds a bit like magic. How do we know to think of creating an imposter here? I won't kid you—there is no formula for flashes of design insight. Ward Cunningham came up with the "trick" a decade ago, and I haven't seen it independently duplicated yet, so it must be a pretty tricky trick. TDD can't guarantee that we will have flashes of insight at the right moment. However, confidence-giving tests and carefully factored code give us preparation for insight, and preparation for applying that insight when it comes.

The solution is to create an object that acts like a Money but represents the sum of two Moneys. I've tried several different metaphors to explain this idea. One is to treat the sum like a *wallet*: you can have several different notes of different denominations and currencies in the same wallet.

Another metaphor is *expression*, as in "(2 + 3) * 5", or in our case "($2 + 3 CHF) * 5". A Money is the atomic form of an expression. Operations result in Expressions, one of which will be a Sum. Once the operation (such as adding up the value of a portfolio) is complete, the resulting Expression can be reduced back to a single currency given a set of exchange rates.

Applying this metaphor to our test, we know what we end up with:

```
public void testSimpleAddition() {
    ...
    assertEquals(Money.dollar(10), reduced);
}
```

The reduced Expression is created by applying exchange rates to an Expression. What in the real world applies exchange rates? A *bank*. We would like to be able to write:

```
public void testSimpleAddition() {
    …
    Money reduced= bank.reduce(sum, "USD");
    assertEquals(Money.dollar(10), reduced);
}
```

(It's a little weird to be mixing the *bank* and *expression* metaphors. We'll get the whole story told first, and then we'll see what we can do about literary value.)

We have made an important design decision here. We could just as easily have written …reduce= sum.reduce("USD", bank). Why make the bank responsible? One answer is, "That's the first thing that popped into my head," but that's not very informative. Why did it pop into my head that reduction should be the responsibility of the bank rather than of the expression? Here's what I'm aware of at the moment:

- Expressions seem to be at the heart of what we are doing. I try to keep the objects at the heart as ignorant of the rest of the world as possible, so they stay flexible as long as possible (and remain easy to test, and reuse, and understand).

- I can imagine there will be many operations involving Expressions. If we add every operation to Expression, then Expression will grow without limit.

That doesn't seem like enough reasons to tip the scales permanently, but it is enough for me to start in this direction. I'm also perfectly willing to move responsibility for reduction to Expression if it turns out that Banks don't need to be involved.

The Bank in our simple example doesn't really need to do anything. As long as we have an object, we're okay:

```
public void testSimpleAddition() {
    …
    Bank bank= new Bank();
    Money reduced= bank.reduce(sum, "USD");
    assertEquals(Money.dollar(10), reduced);
}
```

The sum of two Moneys should be an Expression:

```
public void testSimpleAddition() {
    …
    Expression sum= five.plus(five);
    Bank bank= new Bank();
    Money reduced= bank.reduce(sum, "USD");
    assertEquals(Money.dollar(10), reduced);
}
```

At least we know for sure how to get five dollars:

```
public void testSimpleAddition() {
    Money five= Money.dollar(5);
    Expression sum= five.plus(five);
    Bank bank= new Bank();
    Money reduced= bank.reduce(sum, "USD");
    assertEquals(Money.dollar(10), reduced);
}
```

How do we get this to compile? We need an interface Expression (we could have a class, but an interface is even lighter weight):

Expression
```
interface Expression
```

Money.plus() needs to return an Expression,

Money
```
Expression plus(Money addend) {
    return new Money(amount + addend.amount, currency);
}
```

which means that Money has to implement Expression (which is easy, as there are no operations yet):

Money
```
class Money implements Expression
```

We need an empty Bank class,

Bank
```
class Bank
```

which stubs out reduce():

Bank
```
Money reduce(Expression source, String to) {
    return null;
}
```

Now it compiles, and fails miserably. Hooray! Progress! We can easily fake the implementation, though:

Bank
```
Money reduce(Expression source, String to) {
    return Money.dollar(10);
}
```

We're back to a green bar, and ready to refactor. First, to review, we

- Reduced a big test to a smaller test that represented progress ($5 + 10 CHF to $5 + $5)

- Thought carefully about the possible metaphors for our computation

- Rewrote our previous test based on our new metaphor

- Got the test to compile quickly

- Made it run

- Looked forward with a bit of trepidation to the refactoring necessary to make the implementation real

Chapter 13

Make It

> $5 + 10 CHF = $10 if rate is 2:1
> **$5 + $5 = $10**

We can't mark our test for $5 + $5 done until we've removed all of the duplication. We don't have code duplication, but we do have data duplication—the $10 in the fake implementation:

Bank
```
Money reduce(Expression source, String to) {
    return Money.dollar(10);
}
```

is really the same as the $5 + $5 in the test:

```
public void testSimpleAddition() {
    Money five= Money.dollar(5);
    Expression sum= five.plus(five);
    Bank bank= new Bank();
    Money reduced= bank.reduce(sum, "USD");
    assertEquals(Money.dollar(10), reduced);
}
```

Before when we've had a fake implementation, it has been obvious how to work backward to the real implementation. It simply has been a matter of replacing constants with variables. This time, however, it's not obvious to me how to work backward. So, even though it feels a little speculative, we'll work forward.

> $5 + 10 CHF = $10 if rate is 2:1
> $5 + $5 = $10
> Return Money from $5 + $5

First, `Money.plus()` needs to return a real `Expression`—a `Sum`, not just a `Money`. (Perhaps later we'll optimize the special case of adding two identical currencies, but that's later.)

The sum of two `Money`s should be a `Sum`:

```
public void testPlusReturnsSum() {
    Money five= Money.dollar(5);
    Expression result= five.plus(five);
    Sum sum= (Sum) result;
    assertEquals(five, sum.augend);
    assertEquals(five, sum.addend);
}
```

(Did you know that the first argument to addition is called the *augend*? I didn't until I was writing this. Geek joy.)

The test above is not one I would expect to live a long time. It is deeply concerned with the implementation of our operation, rather than its externally visible behavior. However, if we make it work, we expect we've moved one step closer to our goal. To get it to compile, all we need is a `Sum` class with two fields, augend and addend:

Sum
```
class Sum {
    Money augend;
    Money addend;
}
```

This gives us a `ClassCastException`, because `Money.plus()` is returning a `Money`, not a `Sum`:

Money
```
Expression plus(Money addend) {
    return new Sum(this, addend);
}
```

`Sum` needs a constructor:

Sum
```
Sum(Money augend, Money addend) {
}
```

And `Sum` needs to be a kind of `Expression`:

Sum
```
class Sum implements Expression
```

Now the system compiles again, but the test is still failing, this time because the Sum constructor is not setting the fields. (We could fake the implementation by initializing the fields, but I said I'd start going faster.)

Sum
```
Sum(Money augend, Money addend) {
    this.augend= augend;
    this.addend= addend;
}
```

Now Bank.reduce() is being passed a Sum. If the currencies in the Sum are all the same, and the target currency is also the same, then the result should be a Money whose amount is the sum of the amounts:

```
public void testReduceSum() {
    Expression sum= new Sum(Money.dollar(3), Money.dollar(4));
    Bank bank= new Bank();
    Money result= bank.reduce(sum, "USD");
    assertEquals(Money.dollar(7), result);
}
```

I carefully chose parameters that would break the existing test. When we reduce a Sum, the result (under these simplified circumstances) should be a Money whose amount is the sum of the amounts of the two Moneys and whose currency is the currency to which we are reducing.

Bank
```
Money reduce(Expression source, String to) {
    Sum sum= (Sum) source;
    int amount= sum.augend.amount + sum.addend.amount;
    return new Money(amount, to);
}
```

This is immediately ugly on two counts:

- The cast. This code should work with any Expression.

- The public fields, and two levels of references at that.

Easy enough to fix. First, we can move the body of the method to Sum and get rid of some of the visible fields. We are "sure" we will need the Bank as a parameter in the future, but this is pure, simple refactoring, so we leave it out. (Actually, just now I put it in because I "knew" I would need it—shame, shame on me.)

Bank
```
Money reduce(Expression source, String to) {
    Sum sum= (Sum) source;
    return sum.reduce(to);
}
```

Sum

```
public Money reduce(String to) {
    int amount= augend.amount + addend.amount;
    return new Money(amount, to);
}
```

> $5 + 10 CHF = $10 if rate is 2:1
> $5 + $5 = $10
> Return Money from $5 + $5
> Bank.reduce(Money)

(Which brings up the point of how we are going to implement, er . . . test Bank.reduce() when the argument is a Money.)

Let's write that test, since the bar is green and there is nothing else obvious to do with the code above:

```
public void testReduceMoney() {
    Bank bank= new Bank();
    Money result= bank.reduce(Money.dollar(1), "USD");
    assertEquals(Money.dollar(1), result);
}
```

Bank

```
Money reduce(Expression source, String to) {
    if (source instanceof Money) return (Money) source;
    Sum sum= (Sum) source;
    return sum.reduce(to);
}
```

Ugly, ugly, ugly. However, we now have a green bar, and refactoring is possible. Any time we are checking classes explicitly, we should be using polymorphism instead. Because Sum implements reduce(String), if Money implemented it, too, we could then add it to the Expression interface.

Bank

```
Money reduce(Expression source, String to) {
    if (source instanceof Money)
        return (Money) source.reduce(to);
    Sum sum= (Sum) source;
    return sum.reduce(to);
}
```

Money

```
public Money reduce(String to) {
    return this;
}
```

If we add reduce(String) to the Expression interface,

Expression
```
Money reduce(String to);
```

then we can eliminate all those ugly casts and class checks:

Bank
```
Money reduce(Expression source, String to) {
    return source.reduce(to);
}
```

I'm not entirely happy with the name of the method being the same in Expression and in Bank, but having different parameter types in each. I've never found a satisfactory general solution to this problem in Java. In languages with keyword parameters, communicating the difference between Bank.reduce(Expression, String) and Expression.reduce(String) is well supported by the language syntax. With positional parameters, it's not so easy to make the code speak for us about how the two are different.

> $5 + 10 CHF = $10 if rate is 2:1
> $5 + $5 = $10
> Return Money from $5 + $5
> ~~Bank.reduce(Money)~~
> Reduce Money with conversion
> Reduce(Bank, String)

Next we'll actually exchange one currency for another. First, to review, we

- Didn't mark a test as done because the duplication had not been eliminated

- Worked forward instead of backward to realize the implementation

- Wrote a test to force the creation of an object we expected to need later (Sum)

- Started implementing faster (the Sum constructor)

- Implemented code with casts in one place, then moved the code where it belonged once the tests were running

- Introduced polymorphism to eliminate explicit class checking

Chapter 14

Change

$5 + 10 CHF = $10 if rate is 2:1
$5 + $5 = $10
Return Money from $5 + $5
~~Bank.reduce(Money)~~
Reduce Money with conversion
Reduce(Bank, String)

Change is worth embracing (especially if you have a book out with "embrace change" in the title). Here, however, we are thinking about a much simpler form of change—we have two francs and we want a dollar. That sounds like a test case already:

```
public void testReduceMoneyDifferentCurrency() {
    Bank bank= new Bank();
    bank.addRate("CHF", "USD", 2);
    Money result= bank.reduce(Money.franc(2), "USD");
    assertEquals(Money.dollar(1), result);
}
```

When I convert francs to dollars, I divide by two. (We're still studiously ignoring all of those nasty numerical problems.) We can make the bar green in one piece of ugliness:

Money
```
public Money reduce(String to) {
    int rate = (currency.equals("CHF") && to.equals("USD"))
        ? 2
        : 1;
    return new Money(amount / rate, to);
}
```

Now, suddenly, Money knows about exchange rates. Yuck. The Bank should be the only place we care about exchange rates. We'll have to pass the Bank as a parameter to Expression.reduce(). (See? We *knew* we would need it, and we were

67

right. In the words of the grandfather in *The Princess Bride*, "You're very clever. . . .") First the caller:

Bank
```
Money reduce(Expression source, String to) {
    return source.reduce(this, to);
}
```

Then the implementors:

Expression
```
Money reduce(Bank bank, String to);
```

Sum
```
public Money reduce(Bank bank, String to) {
    int amount= augend.amount + addend.amount;
    return new Money(amount, to);
}
```

Money
```
public Money reduce(Bank bank, String to) {
    int rate = (currency.equals("CHF") && to.equals("USD"))
    ? 2
    : 1;
    return new Money(amount / rate, to);
}
```

The methods have to be public because methods in interfaces have to be public (for some excellent reason, I'm sure).

Now we can calculate the rate in the Bank:

Bank
```
int rate(String from, String to) {
    return (from.equals("CHF") && to.equals("USD"))
    ? 2
    : 1;
}
```

And ask the bank for the right rate:

Money
```
public Money reduce(Bank bank, String to) {
    int rate = bank.rate(currency, to);
    return new Money(amount / rate, to);
}
```

That pesky 2 still appears in both the test and the code. To get rid of it, we need to keep a table of rates in the Bank and look up a rate when we need it. We could use a hashtable that maps pairs of currencies to rates. Can we use a two-element array containing the two currencies as the key? Does Array.equals() check to see if the elements are equal?

```
public void testArrayEquals() {
    assertEquals(new Object[] {"abc"}, new Object[] {"abc"});
}
```

Nope. The test fails, so we have to create a real object for the key:

Pair
```
private class Pair {
    private String from;
    private String to;

    Pair(String from, String to) {
    this.from= from;
    this.to= to;
    }
}
```

Because we are using Pairs as keys, we have to implement equals() and hash-Code(). I'm not going to write tests for these, because we are writing this code in the context of a refactoring. If we get to the payoff of the refactoring and all of the tests run, then we expect the code to have been exercised. If I were programming with someone who didn't see exactly where we were going with this, or if the logic became the least bit complex, I would begin writing separate tests.

Pair
```
public boolean equals(Object object) {
    Pair pair= (Pair) object;
    return from.equals(pair.from) && to.equals(pair.to);
}

public int hashCode() {
    return 0;
}
```

0 is a terrible hash value, but it has the advantage of being easy to implement, and it will get us running quickly. Currency lookup will look like linear search. Later, when we get lots of currencies, we can do a more thorough job with real usage data.

We need somewhere to store the rates:

Bank
```
private Hashtable rates= new Hashtable();
```

We need to set the rate when told:

Bank

```
void addRate(String from, String to, int rate) {
    rates.put(new Pair(from, to), new Integer(rate));
}
```

And then we can look up the rate when asked:

Bank

```
int rate(String from, String to) {
    Integer rate= (Integer) rates.get(new Pair(from, to));
    return rate.intValue();
}
```

Wait a minute! We got a red bar. What happened? A little snooping around tells us that if we ask for the rate from USD to USD, we expect the value to be 1. Because this was a surprise, let's write a test to communicate what we discovered:

```
public void testIdentityRate() {
    assertEquals(1, new Bank().rate("USD", "USD"));
}
```

Now we have three errors, but we expect them all to be fixed with one change:

Bank

```
int rate(String from, String to) {
    if (from.equals(to)) return 1;
    Integer rate= (Integer) rates.get(new Pair(from, to));
    return rate.intValue();
}
```

Green bar!

> $5 + 10 CHF = $10 if rate is 2:1
> ~~$5 + $5 = $10~~
> Return Money from $5 + $5
> ~~Bank.reduce(Money)~~
> ~~Reduce Money with conversion~~
> ~~Reduce(Bank, String)~~

Next we'll implement our last big test, $5 + 10 CHF. Several significant techniques have slipped into this chapter. For now, to review, we

- Added a parameter, in seconds, that we expected we would need

- Factored out the data duplication between code and tests

- Wrote a test (testArrayEquals) to check an assumption about the operation of Java

- Introduced a private helper class without distinct tests of its own

- Made a mistake in a refactoring and chose to forge ahead, writing another test to isolate the problem

Chapter 15

Mixed Currencies

$5 + 10 CHF = $10 if rate is 2:1
~~$5 + $5 = $10~~
Return Money from $5 + $5
~~Bank.reduce(Money)~~
~~Reduce Money with conversion~~
~~Reduce(Bank, String)~~

Now we are finally ready to add the test that started it all, $5 + 10 CHF:

```
public void testMixedAddition() {
    Expression fiveBucks= Money.dollar(5);
    Expression tenFrancs= Money.franc(10);
    Bank bank= new Bank();
    bank.addRate("CHF", "USD", 2);
    Money result= bank.reduce(fiveBucks.plus(tenFrancs), "USD");
    assertEquals(Money.dollar(10), result);
}
```

This is what we'd like to write. Unfortunately, there are a host of compile errors. When we were generalizing from Money to Expression, we left a lot of loose ends laying around. I was worried about them, but I didn't want to disturb you. It's time to disturb you now.

We won't be able to get the preceding test to compile quickly. We will make the first change that will ripple to the next and the next. We have two paths forward. We can make it work quickly by writing a more specific test and then generalizing, or we can trust our compiler not to let us make mistakes. I'm with you—let's go slow (in practice, I would probably just fix the rippling changes one at a time).

```
public void testMixedAddition() {
    Money fiveBucks= Money.dollar(5);
    Money tenFrancs= Money.franc(10);
    Bank bank= new Bank();
```

```
   bank.addRate("CHF", "USD", 2);
   Money result= bank.reduce(fiveBucks.plus(tenFrancs), "USD");
   assertEquals(Money.dollar(10), result);
}
```

The test doesn't work. We get 15 USD instead of 10 USD. It's as if Sum.reduce() weren't reducing the arguments. It isn't:

Sum
```
public Money reduce(Bank bank, String to) {
   int amount= augend.amount + addend.amount;
   return new Money(amount, to);
}
```

If we reduce both of the arguments, the test should pass:

Sum
```
public Money reduce(Bank bank, String to) {
   int amount= augend.reduce(bank, to).amount
      + addend.reduce(bank, to).amount;
   return new Money(amount, to);
}
```

And it does. Now we can begin pecking away at Moneys that should be Expressions. To avoid the ripple effect, we'll start at the edges and work our way back to the test case. For example, the augend and addend can now be Expressions:

Sum
```
Expression augend;
Expression addend;
```

The arguments to the Sum constructor can also be Expressions:

Sum
```
Sum(Expression augend, Expression addend) {
   this.augend= augend;
   this.addend= addend;
}
```

(Sum is starting to remind me of Composite, but not so much that I want to generalize. The moment we want a Sum with other than two parameters, though, I'm ready to transform it.) So much for Sum—how about Money?

The argument to plus() can be an Expression:

Money
```
Expression plus(Expression addend) {
   return new Sum(this, addend);
}
```

Times() can return an Expression:

Money
```
Expression times(int multiplier) {
    return new Money(amount * multiplier, currency);
}
```

This suggests that Expression should include the operations plus() and times(). That's all for Money. We can now change the argument to plus() in our test case:

```
public void testMixedAddition() {
    Money fiveBucks= Money.dollar(5);
    Expression tenFrancs= Money.franc(10);
    Bank bank= new Bank();
    bank.addRate("CHF", "USD", 2);
    Money result= bank.reduce(fiveBucks.plus(tenFrancs), "USD");
    assertEquals(Money.dollar(10), result);
}
```

When we change fiveBucks to an Expression, we have to make several changes. Fortunately we have the compiler's to-do list to keep us focused. First we make the change:

```
public void testMixedAddition() {
    Expression fiveBucks= Money.dollar(5);
    Expression tenFrancs= Money.franc(10);
    Bank bank= new Bank();
    bank.addRate("CHF", "USD", 2);
    Money result= bank.reduce(fiveBucks.plus(tenFrancs), "USD");
    assertEquals(Money.dollar(10), result);
}
```

We are politely told that plus() is not defined for Expressions. We define it:

Expression
```
Expression plus(Expression addend);
```

And then we have to add it to Money and Sum. Money? Yes, it has to be public in Money:

Money
```
public Expression plus(Expression addend) {
    return new Sum(this, addend);
}
```

We'll just stub out the implementation in Sum, and add it to our to-do list:

Sum
```
public Expression plus(Expression addend) {
    return null;
}
```

~~$5 + 10 CHF = $10 if rate is 2:1~~
~~$5 + $5 = $10~~
Return Money from $5 + $5
~~Bank.reduce(Money)~~
~~Reduce Money with conversion~~
~~Reduce(Bank, String)~~
Sum.plus
Expression.times

Now that the program compiles, the tests all run.

We are ready to finish generalizing Money to Expression. But first, to review, we

- Wrote the test we wanted, then backed off to make it achievable in one step

- Generalized (used a more abstract declaration) from the leaves back to the root (the test case)

- Followed the compiler when we made a change (Expression fiveBucks), which caused changes to ripple (added plus() to Expression, and so on)

Chapter 16

Abstraction, Finally

We need to implement Sum.plus() to finish Expression.plus, and then we need Expression.times(), and then we're finished with the whole example. Here's the test for Sum.plus():

```
public void testSumPlusMoney() {
   Expression fiveBucks= Money.dollar(5);
   Expression tenFrancs= Money.franc(10);
   Bank bank= new Bank();
   bank.addRate("CHF", "USD", 2);
   Expression sum= new Sum(fiveBucks, tenFrancs).plus(fiveBucks);
   Money result= bank.reduce(sum, "USD");
   assertEquals(Money.dollar(15), result);
}
```

We could have created a Sum by adding fiveBucks and tenFrancs, but the form above, in which we explicitly create the Sum, communicates more directly. We are writing these tests not just to make our experience of programming more fun and rewarding, but also as a Rosetta stone for future generations to appreciate our genius. Think, oh think, of our readers.

The test, in this case, is longer than the code. The code is the same as the code in Money. (Do I hear an abstract class in the distance?)

Sum
```
public Expression plus(Expression addend) {
   return new Sum(this, addend);
}
```

~~$5 + 10 CHF = $10 if rate is 2:1~~
~~$5 + $5 = $10~~
Return Money from $5 + $5
~~Bank.reduce(Money)~~
~~Reduce Money with conversion~~
~~Reduce(Bank, String)~~
~~Sum.plus~~
Expression.times

You will likely end up with about the same number of lines of test code as model code when implementing TDD. For TDD to make economic sense, you'll need to be able to either write twice as many lines per day as before, or write half as many lines for the same functionality. You'll have to measure and see what effect TDD has on your own practice. Be sure to factor debugging, integrating, and explaining time into your metrics, though.

~~$5 + 10 CHF = $10 if rate is 2:1~~
~~$5 + $5 = $10~~
Return Money from $5 + $5
~~Bank.reduce(Money)~~
~~Reduce Money with conversion~~
~~Reduce(Bank, String)~~
~~Sum.plus~~
Expression.times

If we can make Sum.times() work, then declaring Expression.times() will be one simple step. The test is:

```
public void testSumTimes() {
    Expression fiveBucks= Money.dollar(5);
    Expression tenFrancs= Money.franc(10);
    Bank bank= new Bank();
    bank.addRate("CHF", "USD", 2);
    Expression sum= new Sum(fiveBucks, tenFrancs).times(2);
    Money result= bank.reduce(sum, "USD");
    assertEquals(Money.dollar(20), result);
}
```

Again, the test is longer than the code. (You JUnit geeks will know how to fix that—the rest of you will have to read Fixture.)

Sum
```
Expression times(int multiplier) {
    return new Sum(augend.times(multiplier),addend.times(multiplier));
}
```

Because we abstracted augend and addend to Expressions in the last chapter, we now have to declare times() in Expression for the code to compile:

Expression
```
Expression times(int multiplier);
```

This forces us to raise the visibility of Money.times() and Sum.times():

Sum
```
public Expression times(int multiplier) {
   return new Sum(augend.times(multiplier),addend.times(multiplier));
}
```

Money
```
public Expression times(int multiplier) {
        return new Money(amount * multiplier, currency);
}
```

> $5 + 10 CHF = $10 if rate is 2:1
> $5 + $5 = $10
> Return Money from $5 + $5
> Bank.reduce(Money)
> Reduce Money with conversion
> Reduce(Bank, String)
> Sum.plus
> Expression.times

And it works.

The only loose end to tie up is to experiment with returning a Money when we add $5 + $5. The test would be:

```
public void testPlusSameCurrencyReturnsMoney() {
   Expression sum= Money.dollar(1).plus(Money.dollar(1));
   assertTrue(sum instanceof Money);
}
```

This test is a little ugly, because it is testing the guts of the implementation, not the externally visible behavior of the objects. However, it will drive us to make the changes we need to make, and this is only an experiment, after all. Here is the code we would have to modify to make it work:

Money
```
public Expression plus(Expression addend) {
   return new Sum(this, addend);
}
```

~~$5 + 10 CHF = $10 if rate is 2:1~~
~~$5 + $5 = $10~~
~~Return Money from $5 + $5~~
~~Bank.reduce(Money)~~
~~Reduce Money with conversion~~
~~Reduce(Bank, String)~~
~~Sum.plus~~
~~Expression.times~~

There is no obvious, clean way (not to me, anyway; I'm sure you could think of something) to check the currency of the argument if and only if it is a Money. The experiment fails, we delete the test (which we didn't like much anyway), and away we go.

To review, we

- Wrote a test with future readers in mind

- Suggested an experiment comparing TDD with your current programming style

- Once again had changes of declarations ripple through the system, and once again followed the compiler's advice to fix them

- Tried a brief experiment, then discarded it when it didn't work out

Chapter 17

Money Retrospective

Let's take a look back at the money example, both the process we used and the results. We will look at:

- What's Next?

- Metaphor—The dramatic effect metaphor has on the structure of the design.

- JUnit Usage—When we ran tests and how we used JUnit.

- Code Metrics—A numerical abstract of the resulting code.

- Process—We say red/green/refactor, but how much work goes into each step?

- Test Quality—How do TDD tests stack up against conventional test metrics?

What's Next?

Is the code finished? No. There is that nasty duplication between Sum.plus() and Money.plus(). If we made Expression a class instead of an interface (not the usual direction, as classes more often become interfaces), we would have a natural home for the common code.

I don't believe in "finished." TDD can be used as a way to strive for perfection, but that isn't its most effective use. If you have a big system, then the parts that you touch all the time should be absolutely rock solid, so you can make daily changes confidently. As you drift out to the periphery of the system, to parts that don't change often, the tests can be spottier and the design uglier without interfering with your confidence.

When I've done all of the obvious tasks, I like running a code critic, like Small-Lint for Smalltalk. Many of the suggestions that come up I already know about, or I disagree with. Automated critics don't forget, however, so if I don't delete an obsolete implementation I don't have to stress. The critic will point it out.

Another "what's next?" question is, "What additional tests do I need?" Sometimes you think of a test that "shouldn't" work, and it does. Then you need to find out why. Sometimes a test that shouldn't work really doesn't, and you can record it as a known limitation or as work to be done later.

Finally, when the list is empty is a good time to review the design. Do the words and concepts play together? Is there duplication that is difficult to eliminate given the current design? (Lingering duplication is a symptom of latent design.)

Metaphor

The biggest surprise for me in coding the money example was how different it came out this time. I have programmed money in production at least three times that I can think of. I have used it as an example in print another half-dozen times. I have programmed it live on stage (relax, it's not as exciting as it sounds) another fifteen times. I coded another three or four times preparing for writing (ripping out Part I and rewriting it based on early reviews). Then, while I was writing this, I thought of using *expression* as the metaphor and the design went in a completely different direction than before.

I really didn't expect the metaphor to be so powerful. A metaphor should just be a source of names, shouldn't it? Apparently not.

The metaphor that Ward Cunningham used for "several monies together with potentially different currencies" was a vector, like a mathematical vector where the coefficients were currencies instead of x^2. I used MoneySum for a while, then MoneyBag (which is nice and physical), and finally Wallet (which is more common in most folks' experience). All of these metaphors imply that the collection of Moneys is flat. For example, "2 USD + 5 CHF + 3 USD" would result in "5 USD + 5 CHF". Two values with the same currency would be merged.

The *expression* metaphor freed me from a bunch of nasty issues about merging duplicated currencies. The code came out cleaner and clearer than I've ever seen it before. I'm concerned about the performance of expressions, but I'm happy to wait until I see some usage statistics before I start optimizing.

What if I got to rewrite everything I ever wrote 20 times? Would I keep finding insight and surprise every time? Is there some way to be more mindful as I program so I can squeeze all the insight out of the first three times? The first time?

JUnit Usage

I had JUnit keep a log while I was coding the money example. I pressed the Run button precisely 125 times. Because I was writing at the same time as I was programming, the interval between runs isn't representative, but during the times I was just programming I ran the tests about once per minute. Only once in that whole time was I surprised by either success or failure, and that was a refactoring done in haste.

Figure 17.1 is a histogram of the time interval between test runs. The large number of long intervals is most likely because of the time I spent writing.

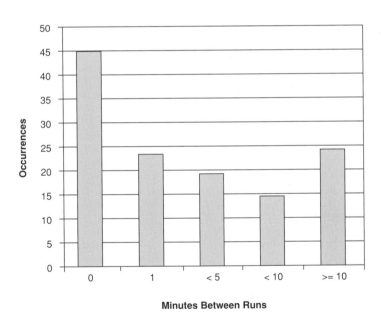

Figure 17.1 *Histogram of the time interval between test runs*

Code Metrics

Table 17.1 gives some statistics about the code.

Table 17.1 *Code Metrics*

	Functional	Test
Classes	5	1
Functions (1)	22	15
Lines (2)	91	89
Cyclomatic complexity (3)	1.04	1
Lines/function	4.1 (4)	5.9 (5)

(1) Because we haven't implemented the whole API, we can't evaluate the absolute number of functions, or the number of functions per class, or the number of lines per class. However, the ratios are instructive. There are roughly as many lines and functions in the test and functional code.

(2) The number of lines of test code can be reduced by extracting common fixtures. The rough correspondence between lines of model code and lines of test code will remain, however.

(3) Cyclomatic complexity is a measure of conventional flow complexity. Test complexity is 1 because there are no branches or loops in test code. Functional code complexity is low because of the heavy use of polymorphism as a substitute for explicit control flow.

(4) This includes the function header and trailing brace.

(5) Lines per function in the tests is inflated because we have not factored out common fixture-building code, as explained in the section JUnit Usage (page 83).

Process

The TDD cycle is as follows.

- Add a little test.
- Run all tests and fail.

- Make a change.

- Run the tests and succeed.

- Refactor to remove duplication.

Assuming that writing a test is a single step, how many changes does it take to compile, run, and refactor? (By change, I mean changing a method or class definition.) Figure 17.2 shows a histogram of the number of changes for each of the money tests you have just seen.

I expect that if we gathered data for a large project, the number of changes to compile and run would remain fairly small (they could be even smaller if the programming environment understood what the tests were trying to tell it—creating stubs automatically, for instance). However, (and here's at least a master's thesis) the number of changes per refactoring should follow a "fat tail" or leptokurtotic profile, which is like a bell curve but with more extreme changes than predicted by a standard bell curve. Many measurements in nature follow this profile, such as price changes in the stock market.[1]

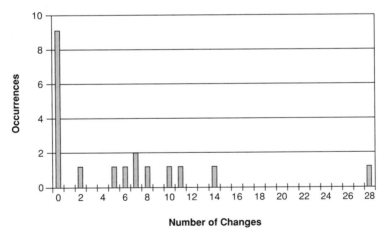

Figure 17.2 *Number of changes per refactoring*

---

1. Mandelbrot, Benoit, ed. 1997. *Fractals and Scaling in Finance.* New York: Springer-Verlag. ISBN: 0387983635

Test Quality

The tests that are a natural by-product of TDD are certainly useful enough to keep running as long as the system is running. Don't expect them to replace the other types of testing:

- Performance

- Stress

- Usability

However, if the defect density of test-driven code is low enough, then the role of professional testing will inevitably change from "adult supervision" to something more closely resembling an amplifier for the communication between those who generally have a feeling for what the system should do and those who will make it do. As a stand-in for a long and interesting conversation about the future of professional testing, here are a couple of widely shared measurements of the tests written above.

- *Statement coverage* certainly is not a sufficient measure of test quality, but it is a starting place. TDD followed religiously should result in 100 percent statement coverage. JProbe (www.sitraka.com/software/jprobe) reports only one line in one method not covered by the test cases—`Money.toString()`, which we added explicitly as a debugging aid, not real model code.

- *Defect insertion* is another way of evaluating test quality. The idea is simple: change the meaning of a line of code and a test should break. You can do this manually, or with a tool such as Jester (jester.sourceforge.net). Jester reports only one line it is able to change without breaking, `Pair.hashCode()`. We faked the implementation to just return 0. Returning a different constant doesn't actually change the meaning of the program (one fake number is as good as another), so it isn't really a defect that has been inserted.

Phlip, one of my reviewers, made a point about test coverage that bears repeating here. A gross measure of coverage is the number of tests testing different aspects of a program divided by the number of aspects that need testing (the complexity of the logic). One way to improve coverage is to write more tests, hence the dramatic difference in the number of tests a test-driven developer would write for code and the number of tests a professional tester would write. (Chapter 32) gives details of an example in which I wrote 6 tests and a tester wrote 65 tests for the same problem.) However, another way to improve coverage is to take a fixed set of tests and simplify the logic of the program. The refactoring step often has this effect—conditionals replaced by messages, or by nothing at all. In Phlip's words, "Instead of increasing the test coverage to walk all permutations of input (more properly an efficiently reduced sample of all possible permutations), we just leave the same tests covering various permutations of code as it shrinks."

One Last Review

The three items that come up time and again as surprises when teaching TDD are:

- The three approaches to making a test work cleanly—fake it, triangulation, and obvious implementation

- Removing duplication between test and code as a way to drive the design

- The ability to control the gap between tests to increase traction when the road gets slippery and cruise faster when conditions are clear

PART II

The xUnit Example

How, oh how, to talk about the implementation of a tool for test-driven development? Test-drive, naturally.

The xUnit architecture comes out very smoothly in Python, so I'll switch to Python for Part II. Don't worry, I'll give a little commentary on Python, for those of you who haven't seen it before. When you're done you'll have an introduction to Python, you'll be able to write your own testing framework, and you'll have seen a trickier example of TDD—three for the price of one.

Chapter 18

First Steps to xUnit

Driving a testing tool using the testing tool itself to run the tests may seem a bit like performing brain surgery on yourself. ("Don't touch those motor centers—oh, too bad, game over.") It will get weird from time to time. However, the logic of the testing framework is more complicated than the wimpy money example of Part I. You can read Part II as a step toward test-driven development of "real" software. You can read it as a computer-sciency exercise in self-referential programming.

First, we need to be able to create a test case and run a test method. For example: TestCase("testMethod").run(). We have a bootstrap problem: we are writing test cases to test a framework that we will be using to write the test cases. Because we don't have a framework yet, we will have to verify the operation of the first tiny step by hand. Fortunately, we are well rested and relaxed and unlikely to make mistakes, which is why we will go in teeny-tiny steps, verifying everything six ways from Sunday. Here is the to-do list that comes to mind for a testing framework.

> **Invoke test method**
> Invoke setUp first
> Invoke tearDown afterward
> Invoke tearDown even if the test method fails
> Run multiple tests
> Report collected results

We are still working test-first, of course. For our first proto-test, we need a little program that will print out true if a test method gets called, and false otherwise. If we have a test case that sets a flag inside the test method, then we can print the flag after we're done and make sure it's correct. Once we have verified it manually, we can automate the process.

Here's the strategy for our bootstrap test: We will create a test case that contains a flag. Before the test method is run, the flag should be false. The test method will set the flag. After the test method is run, the flag should be true. We'll call the TestCase class WasRun, because it's a test case that reports whether a method was run. The flag will also be called wasRun (perhaps confusing, but it's such a good name), so we can eventually write assert test.wasRun (assert is a built-in Python facility).

Python executes statements as it reads a file, so we can start by invoking the test method manually:

```
test= WasRun("testMethod")
print test.wasRun
test.testMethod()
print test.wasRun
```

We expect this to print "None" before the method was run, and "1" afterward. (None in Python is like null or nil, and stands for *false*, along with 0 and a few other objects.) But it doesn't do what we expect, because we haven't defined the class WasRun yet (test-*first*, test-*first*).

WasRun
```
class WasRun:
    pass
```

(The keyword pass is used when there is no implementation of a class or method.) Now we are told we need an attribute wasRun. We need to create the attribute when we create the instance (the constructor is called __init__ for convenience). In it, we set the wasRun flag to false.

WasRun
```
class WasRun:
    def __init__(self, name):
    self.wasRun= None
```

Running the file faithfully prints out "None", then tells us we need to define the method testMethod. (Wouldn't it be great if your IDE noticed this, provided you with a stub, and opened up an editor on it? Nah, too useful.)

WasRun
```
def testMethod(self):
    pass
```

Now when we execute the file, we see "None" and "None". We want to see "None" and "1". We can get it by setting the flag in testMethod():

WasRun
```
def testMethod(self):
    self.wasRun= 1
```

Now we get the right answer—the green bar, hooray! We have a bunch of refactoring to do, but as long as we maintain the green bar, we know we have made progress.

Next we need to use our real interface, run(), instead of calling the test method directly. The test changes to the following:

```
test= WasRun("testMethod")
print test.wasRun
test.run()
print test.wasRun
```

The implementation we can hardwire at the moment to:

WasRun
```
def run(self):
    self.testMethod()
```

And our test is back to printing the right values again. Lots of refactoring has this feel—separating two parts so you can work on them separately. If they go back together when you are finished, fine; if not, you can leave them separate. In this case, we expect to create a superclass TestCase, eventually, but first we have to differentiate the parts of our one example. There is probably some clever analogy with mitosis in here, but I don't know enough cellular biology to explain it.

The next step is to dynamically invoke the testMethod. One of the coolest features of Python is that items like the names of classes and methods can be treated like functions (see the invocation of WasRun above). When we get the attribute corresponding to the name of the test case, we are returned an object which, when invoked as a function, invokes the method.[1]

WasRun
```
class WasRun:
    def __init__(self, name):
        self.wasRun= None
        self.name= name
    def run(self):
        method = getattr(self, self.name)
        method()
```

Here is another general pattern of refactoring: take code that works in one instance and generalize it to work in many by replacing constants with variables. Here the constant was hardwired code, not a data value, but the principle is the same. TDD makes this work well by giving you running concrete

---

1. Thanks to Duncan Booth for correcting my Python newbie mistake and suggesting the Pythonic solution.

examples from which to generalize, instead of having to generalize purely with reasoning.

Now our little WasRun class is doing two distinct jobs: one is keeping track of whether a method was invoked or not, and the other is dynamically invoking the method. Time for a little of that mitosis action. First we create an empty TestCase superclass, and make WasRun a subclass:

TestCase
```
class TestCase:
    pass
```

WasRun
```
class WasRun(TestCase): . . .
```

Now we can move the name attribute up to the superclass:

TestCase
```
def __init__(self, name):
    self.name= name
```

WasRun
```
def __init__(self, name):
    self.wasRun= None
    TestCase.__init__(self, name)
```

Finally, the run() method uses attributes from the superclass only, so it probably belongs in the superclass. (I'm always looking to put the operations near the data.)

TestCase
```
def __init__(self, name):
    self.name= name
def run(self):
    method = getattr(self, self.name)
    method()
```

Between every one of these steps, I run the tests to make sure I'm getting the same answer.

We're getting tired of looking to see that "None" and "1" are printed every time. Using the mechanism we just built, we can now write:

TestCaseTest
```
class TestCaseTest(TestCase):
    def testRunning(self):
        test= WasRun("testMethod")
        assert(not test.wasRun)
        test.run()
        assert(test.wasRun)
TestCaseTest("testRunning").run()
```

~~Invoke test method~~
Invoke setUp first
Invoke tearDown afterward
Invoke tearDown even if the test method fails
Run multiple tests
Report collected results

The body of the test is just the print statements turned into assertions, so you could just see what we have done as a complicated form of Extract Method.

I'll let you in on a little secret. I look at the size of the steps in the development I've just shown you, and it looks ridiculous. On the other hand, I tried it with bigger steps, spending probably six hours in all (I had to spend a lot of time looking up Python stuff) and starting from scratch twice, and both times I thought I had the code working when I didn't. This is about the worst possible case for TDD, because we are trying to get over the bootstrap step.

It is not necessary to work in such tiny steps as these. Once you've mastered TDD, you will be able to work in much bigger leaps of functionality between test cases. However, to master TDD you need to be able to work in such tiny steps when they are called for.

Next we will tackle calling setUp() before running the test. To review first, we

- After a couple of hubris-fueled false starts, figured out how to begin with a tiny little step

- Implemented functionality, by first hardwiring it, and then making it more general by replacing constants with variables

- Used Pluggable Selector, which we promise not to use again for four months, minimum, because it makes code hard to analyze statically

- Bootstrapped our testing framework, all in tiny steps

Chapter 19

Set the Table

When you begin writing tests, you will discover a common pattern (Bill Wake coined the term *3A* for this).

1. Arrange—Create some objects.

2. Act—Stimulate them.

3. Assert—Check the results.

> ~~Invoke test method~~
> **Invoke setUp first**
> Invoke tearDown afterward
> Invoke tearDown even if the test method fails
> Run multiple tests
> Report collected results

The first step, arrange, is often the same from test to test, whereas the second and third steps, act and assert, are unique. I have a 7 and a 9. If I add them, I expect 16; if I subtract them, I expect –2; and if I multiply them, I expect 63. The stimulation and expected results are unique, but the 7 and the 9 don't change.

If this pattern repeats at different scales (and it does), then we're faced with the question of how often do we want to create new objects to test. Two constraints come into conflict.

- Performance—We would like our tests to run as quickly as possible; namely, if we use similar objects in several tests, we would like to create them once for all tests.

- Isolation—We would like the success or failure of one test to be irrelevant to other tests. If tests share objects and one test changes the objects, following tests are likely to change their results.

Test coupling has an obvious nasty effect, in that breaking one test causes the next ten to fail even though the code is correct. Test coupling can have a subtle but very nasty effect, in situations in which the order of tests matters: If I run test A before test B, they both work, but if I run test B before test A, then test A fails. Or even nastier, the code exercised by test B is wrong, but because test A ran first, the test passes.

Test coupling—don't go there. Let's assume for the moment that we can make object creation go fast enough. In this case, we would like to create the objects for a test every time the test runs. We've already seen a disguised form of this in WasRun, where we wanted to have a flag set to false before we ran the test. Taking steps toward this, first we need a test:

TestCaseTest
```
def testSetUp(self):
    test= WasRun("testMethod")
    test.run()
    assert(test.wasSetUp)
```

Running this (by adding the last line TestCaseTest("testSetUp").run() to our file), Python politely informs us that there is no wasSetUp attribute. Of course not. We haven't set it. This method should do it:

WasRun
```
def setUp(self):
    self.wasSetUp= 1
```

It would if we were calling it. Calling setUp is the job of the TestCase, so we turn there:

TestCase
```
def setUp(self):
    pass
def run(self):
    self.setUp()
    method = getattr(self, self.name)
    method()
```

That's two steps to get a test case running, which is too many in such ticklish circumstances. We'll see if it will work. Yes, it does pass. However, if you want to learn something, try to figure out how we could have gotten the test to pass by changing no more than one method at a time.

We can immediately use our new facility to shorten our tests. First, we can simplify WasRun by setting the wasRun flag in setUp:

WasRun
```
def setUp(self):
    self.wasRun= None
    self.wasSetUp= 1
```

We have to simplify testRunning not to check the flag before running the test. Are we willing to give up this much confidence in our code? Only if testSetUp is in place. This is a common pattern—one test can be simple if and only if another test is in place and running correctly:

TestCaseTest
```
def testRunning(self):
    test= WasRun("testMethod")
    test.run()
    assert(test.wasRun)
```

We can also simplify the tests themselves. In both cases we create an instance of WasRun, exactly that fixture we were talking about earlier. We can create the WasRun in setUp, and use it in the test methods. Each test method is run in a clean instance of TestCaseTest, so there is no way the two tests can be coupled. (We're assuming that the objects don't interact in some incredibly ugly way, like setting global variables, but we wouldn't do that, not with all those other readers watching.)

TestCaseTest
```
def setUp(self):
    self.test= WasRun("testMethod")
def testRunning(self):
    self.test.run()
    assert(self.test.wasRun)
def testSetUp(self):
    self.test.run()
    assert(self.test.wasSetUp)
```

~~Invoke test method~~
~~Invoke setUp first~~
Invoke tearDown afterward
Invoke tearDown even if the test method fails
Run multiple tests
Report collected results

Next we'll run tearDown() after the test method. To review this chapter, we

- Decided that simplicity of test writing was more important than performance for the moment

- Tested and implemented setUp()

- Used setUp() to simplify the example test case

- Used setUp() to simplify the test cases checking the example test case (I told you this would become like self-brain-surgery.)

Chapter 20

Cleaning Up After

~~Invoke test method~~
~~Invoke setUp first~~
Invoke tearDown afterward
Invoke tearDown even if the test method fails
Run multiple tests
Report collected results

Sometimes tests need to allocate external resources in setUp(). If we want the tests to remain independent, then a test that allocates external resources needs to release them before it is done, perhaps in a tearDown() method.

The simpleminded way to write the test for de-allocation is to introduce yet another flag. All of those flags are starting to bug me, and they are missing an important aspect of the methods: setUp() is called before the test method is run, and tearDown() is called afterward. I'm going to change the testing strategy to keep a little log of the methods that are called. By always appending to the log, we will preserve the order in which the methods are called.

~~Invoke test method~~
~~Invoke setUp first~~
Invoke tearDown afterward
Invoke tearDown even if the test method fails
Run multiple tests
Report collected results
Log string in WasRun

WasRun
```
def setUp(self):
    self.wasRun= None
    self.wasSetUp= 1
    self.log= "setUp "
```

101

Now we can change testSetUp() to look at the log instead of the flag:

TestCaseTest
```
def testSetUp(self):
    self.test.run()
    assert("setUp " == self.test.log)
```

Next we can delete the wasSetUp flag. We can record the running of the test method, too:

WasRun
```
def testMethod(self):
    self.wasRun= 1
    self.log= self.log + "testMethod "
```

This breaks testSetUp, because the actual log contains "setUp testMethod ". We change the expected value:

TestCaseTest
```
def testSetUp(self):
    self.test.run()
    assert("setUp testMethod " == self.test.log)
```

Now this test is doing the work of both tests, so we can delete testRunning and rename testSetUp:

TestCaseTest
```
def setUp(self):
    self.test= WasRun("testMethod")
def testTemplateMethod(self):
    self.test.run()
    assert("setUp testMethod " == self.test.log)
```

Unfortunately, we are using the instance if WasRun in only one place, so we have to undo our clever setUp hack:

TestCaseTest
```
def testTemplateMethod(self):
    test= WasRun("testMethod")
    test.run()
    assert("setUp testMethod " == test.log)
```

Doing a refactoring based on a couple of early uses, then having to undo it soon after is fairly common. Some folks wait until they have three or four uses before refactoring because they don't like undoing work. I prefer to spend my thinking cycles on design, so I just reflexively do the refactorings without worrying about whether I will have to undo them immediately afterward.

~~Invoke test method~~
~~Invoke setUp first~~
Invoke tearDown afterward
Invoke tearDown even if the test method fails
Run multiple tests
Report collected results
~~Log string in WasRun~~

Now we are ready to implement tearDown(). Got you! Now we are ready to test for tearDown:

TestCaseTest

```
def testTemplateMethod(self):
    test= WasRun("testMethod")
    test.run()
    assert("setUp testMethod tearDown " == test.log)
```

This fails. Making it work is simple:

TestCase

```
def run(self, result):
    result.testStarted()
    self.setUp()
    method = getattr(self, self.name)
    method()
    self.tearDown()
```

WasRun

```
def setUp(self):
    self.log= "setUp "
def testMethod(self):
    self.log= self.log + "testMethod "
def tearDown(self):
    self.log= self.log + "tearDown "
```

Surprisingly, we get an error, not in WasRun, but in the TestCaseTest. We don't have a no-op implementation of tearDown() in TestCase:

TestCase

```
def tearDown(self):
    pass
```

This time we got value out of using the same testing framework we are developing. Yippee! No refactoring necessary. The Obvious Implementation, after that one glitch, worked and was clean.

~~Invoke test method~~
~~Invoke setUp first~~
~~Invoke tearDown afterward~~
Invoke tearDown even if the test method fails
Run multiple tests
Report collected results
~~Log string in WasRun~~

Next we'll go on to report the results of running a test explicitly, instead of letting Python's native error handling and reporting system tell us when there is a problem with an assertion. To review, in this chapter, we

- Restructured the testing strategy from flags to a log

- Tested and implemented `tearDown()` using the new log

- Found a problem and, daringly, fixed it instead of backing up (Was that a good idea?)

Chapter 21

Counting

Invoke test method
Invoke setUp first
Invoke tearDown afterward
Invoke tearDown even if the test method fails
Run multiple tests
Report collected results
Log string in WasRun

I was going to include an implementation to ensure that tearDown() is called regardless of exceptions during the test method. However, we need to catch exceptions in order to make the test work. (I know, I just tried it, and backed it out.) If we make a mistake implementing this, then we won't be able to see the mistake because the exceptions won't be reported.

In general, the order of implementing the tests is important. When I pick the next test to implement, I find a test that will teach me something and which I have confidence I can make work. If I get that test working but get stuck on the next one, then I consider backing up two steps. It would be great if the programming environment helped me with this, working as a checkpoint for the code every time all of the tests run.

We would like to see the results of running any number of tests—"5 run, 2 failed, TestCaseTest.testFooBar—ZeroDivideException, MoneyTest.testNegation—AssertionError". Then if the tests stop getting called, or if results stop getting reported, at least we have a chance of catching the error. Having the framework automatically report all of the test cases it knows nothing about seems a bit farfetched, at least for the first test case.

We'll have TestCase.run() return a TestResult object that records the results of running the test (singular for the moment, but we'll get to that).

TestCaseTest
```
def testResult(self):
    test= WasRun("testMethod")
    result= test.run()
    assert("1 run, 0 failed" == result.summary())
```

We'll start with a fake implementation:

TestResult
```
class TestResult:
    def summary(self):
        return "1 run, 0 failed"
```

and return a TestResult as the result of TestCase.run()

TestCase
```
def run(self):
    self.setUp()
    method = getattr(self, self.name)
    method()
    self.tearDown()
    return TestResult()
```

Now that the test runs, we can realize (as in "make real") the implementation of summary() a little at a time. First, we can make the number of tests run a symbolic constant:

TestResult
```
def __init__(self):
    self.runCount= 1
def summary(self):
    return "%d run, 0 failed" % self.runCount
```

(The % operator is Python's sprintf.) However, runCount shouldn't be a constant; it should be computed by counting the number of tests run. We can initialize it to 0, then increment it every time a test is run.

TestResult
```
def __init__(self):
    self.runCount= 0
def testStarted(self):
    self.runCount= self.runCount + 1
def summary(self):
    return "%d run, 0 failed" % self.runCount
```

We have to actually call this groovy new method:

TestCase
```
def run(self):
    result= TestResult()
    result.testStarted()
    self.setUp()
    method = getattr(self, self.name)
    method()
    self.tearDown()
    return result
```

We could turn the constant string "0" for the number of failed tests into a variable in the same way as we realized runCount, but the tests don't demand it. So instead we write another test:

TestCaseTest
```
def testFailedResult(self):
    test= WasRun("testBrokenMethod")
    result= test.run()
    assert("1 run, 1 failed", result.summary)
```

where:

WasRun
```
def testBrokenMethod(self):
    raise Exception
```

~~Invoke test method~~
~~Invoke setUp first~~
~~Invoke tearDown afterward~~
Invoke tearDown even if the test method fails
Run multiple tests
~~Report collected results~~
~~Log string in WasRun~~
Report failed tests

The first thing we notice is that we aren't catching the exception thrown by WasRun.testBrokenMethod. We would like to catch the exception and make a note in the result that the test failed. We'll put this test on the shelf for the moment.

To review, we

- Wrote a fake implementation, and gradually began making it real by replacing constants with variables

- Wrote another test

- When that test failed, wrote yet another test, at a smaller scale, to support making the failing test work

Chapter 22

Dealing with Failure

<del>Invoke test method</del>
<del>Invoke setUp first</del>
<del>Invoke tearDown afterward</del>
Invoke tearDown even if the test method fails
Run multiple tests
<del>Report collected results</del>
<del>Log string in WasRun</del>
Report failed tests

We'll write a smaller grained test to ensure that if we note a failed test, we print out the right results:

TestCaseTest
```
def testFailedResultFormatting(self):
    result= TestResult()
    result.testStarted()
    result.testFailed()
    assert("1 run, 1 failed" == result.summary())
```

"testStarted()" and "testFailed()" are the messages we expect to send to the result when a test starts and when a test fails, respectively. If we can get the summary to print correctly when these messages are sent in this order, then our programming problem is reduced to how to get these messages sent. Once they are sent, we expect the whole thing to work.

The implementation is to keep a count of failures:

TestResult
```
def __init__(self):
    self.runCount= 0
    self.errorCount= 0
def testFailed(self):
    self.errorCount= self.errorCount + 1
```

109

With the count correct (which I suppose we could have tested for, if we were taking teensy, weensy, tiny steps—but I won't bother, the coffee has kicked in now), we can print correctly:

TestResult
```
def summary(self):
    return "%d run, %d failed" % (self.runCount, self.failureCount)
```

Now we expect that if we call testFailed() correctly, then we will get the expected answer. When do we call it? When we catch an exception in the test method:

TestCase
```
def run(self):
    result= TestResult()
    result.testStarted()
    self.setUp()
    try:
        method = getattr(self, self.name)
        method()
    except:
        result.testFailed()
    self.tearDown()
    return result
```

There is a subtlety hidden inside this method. The way it is written, if a disaster happens during setUp(), then the exception won't be caught. That can't be what we mean—we want our tests to run independently of one another. However, we need another test before we can change the code. (I taught Bethany, my oldest daughter, TDD as her first programming style when she was about age 12. She thinks you can't type in code unless there is a broken test. The rest of us have to muddle through reminding ourselves to write the tests.) I'll leave that next test and its implementation as an exercise for you (sore fingers, again).

~~Invoke test method~~
~~Invoke setUp first~~
~~Invoke tearDown afterward~~
Invoke tearDown even if the test method fails
Run multiple tests
~~Report collected results~~
~~Log string in WasRun~~
~~Report failed tests~~
Catch and report setUp errors

Next we will work on getting several tests to run together. To review this chapter, we

- Made our small-scale test work

- Reintroduced the larger scale test

- Made the larger test work quickly using the mechanism demonstrated by the smaller test

- Noticed a potential problem and noted it on the to-do list instead of addressing it immediately

Chapter 23

How Suite It Is

~~Invoke test method~~
~~Invoke setUp first~~
~~Invoke tearDown afterward~~
Invoke tearDown even if the test method fails
Run multiple tests
~~Report collected results~~
~~Log string in WasRun~~
~~Report failed tests~~
Catch and report setUp errors

We can't leave xUnit without visiting TestSuite. The end of our file, where we invoke all of the tests, is looking pretty ratty:

```
print TestCaseTest("testTemplateMethod").run().summary()
print TestCaseTest("testResult").run().summary()
print TestCaseTest("testFailedResultFormatting").run().summary()
print TestCaseTest("testFailedResult").run().summary()
```

Duplication is always a bad thing, unless you look at it as motivation to find the missing design element. Here we would like the ability to compose tests and run them together. (Working hard to make tests run in isolation doesn't do us much good if we only ever run one at a time.) Another good reason to implement TestSuite is that it gives us a pure example of Composite—we want to be able to treat single tests and groups of tests exactly the same.

We would like to be able to create a TestSuite, add a few tests to it, and then get collective results from running it:

TestCaseTest
```
def testSuite(self):
    suite= TestSuite()
    suite.add(WasRun("testMethod"))
    suite.add(WasRun("testBrokenMethod"))
    result= suite.run()
    assert("2 run, 1 failed" == result.summary())
```

113

Implementing the add() method merely adds tests to a list:

TestSuite
```
class TestSuite:
    def __init__(self):
        self.tests= []
    def add(self, test):
        self.tests.append(test)
```

(Python note: [] creates an empty collection.)

The run method is a bit of a problem. We want a single TestResult to be used by all of the tests that run. Therefore, we should write:

TestSuite
```
def run(self):
    result= TestResult()
    for test in tests:
        test.run(result)
    return result
```

(Python note: for test in tests iterates through the elements of tests, assigning each one to test and evaluating the following code.) However, one of the main constraints on Composite is that the collection must respond to the same messages as the individual items. If we add a parameter to TestCase.run(), then we have to add the same parameter to TestSuite.run(). I can think of three alternatives:

- Use Python's default parameter mechanism. Unfortunately, the default value is evaluated at compile time, not run time, and we don't want to be reusing the same TestResult.

- Split the method into two parts—one that allocates the TestResult and another which runs the test given a TestResult. I can't think of good names for the two parts of the method, which suggests that this isn't a good strategy.

- Allocate the TestResults in the caller.

We will allocate the TestResults in the callers. This pattern is called Collecting Parameter.

TestCaseTest
```
def testSuite(self):
    suite= TestSuite()
    suite.add(WasRun("testMethod"))
    suite.add(WasRun("testBrokenMethod"))
    result= TestResult()
    suite.run(result)
    assert("2 run, 1 failed" == result.summary())
```

This solution has the advantage that run() now has no explicit return:

TestSuite
```
def run(self, result):
    for test in tests:
        test.run(result)
```

TestCase
```
def run(self, result):
    result.testStarted()
    self.setUp()
    try:
        method = getattr(self, self.name)
        method()
    except:
        result.testFailed()
    self.tearDown()
```

Now we can clean up the invocation of the tests at the end of the file:

```
suite= TestSuite()
suite.add(TestCaseTest("testTemplateMethod"))
suite.add(TestCaseTest("testResult"))
suite.add(TestCaseTest("testFailedResultFormatting"))
suite.add(TestCaseTest("testFailedResult"))
suite.add(TestCaseTest("testSuite"))
result= TestResult()
suite.run(result)
print result.summary()
```

~~Invoke test method~~
~~Invoke setUp first~~
~~Invoke tearDown afterward~~
Invoke tearDown even if the test method fails
Run multiple tests
~~Report collected results~~
~~Log string in WasRun~~
~~Report failed tests~~
Catch and report setUp errors
Create TestSuite from a TestCase class

There is substantial duplication here, which we could eliminate if we had a way of constructing a suite automatically given a test class.

However, first we have to fix the four failing tests (they use the old no-argument run interface):

TestCaseTest

```
def testTemplateMethod(self):
    test= WasRun("testMethod")
    result= TestResult()
    test.run(result)
    assert("setUp testMethod tearDown " == test.log)
def testResult(self):
    test= WasRun("testMethod")
    result= TestResult()
    test.run(result)
    assert("1 run, 0 failed" == result.summary())
def testFailedResult(self):
    test= WasRun("testBrokenMethod")
    result= TestResult()
    test.run(result)
    assert("1 run, 1 failed" == result.summary())
def testFailedResultFormatting(self):
    result= TestResult()
    result.testStarted()
    result.testFailed()
    assert("1 run, 1 failed" == result.summary())
```

Notice that each test allocates a TestResult, exactly the problem solved by setUp(). We can simplify the tests (at the cost of making them a little more difficult to read) by creating the TestResult in setUp():

TestCaseTest

```
def setUp(self):
    self.result= TestResult()
def testTemplateMethod(self):
    test= WasRun("testMethod")
    test.run(self.result)
    assert("setUp testMethod tearDown " == test.log)
def testResult(self):
    test= WasRun("testMethod")
    test.run(self.result)
    assert("1 run, 0 failed" == self.result.summary())
def testFailedResult(self):
    test= WasRun("testBrokenMethod")
    test.run(self.result)
    assert("1 run, 1 failed" == self.result.summary())
def testFailedResultFormatting(self):
    self.result.testStarted()
    self.result.testFailed()
    assert("1 run, 1 failed" == self.result.summary())
def testSuite(self):
    suite= TestSuite()
    suite.add(WasRun("testMethod"))
```

```
suite.add(WasRun("testBrokenMethod"))
suite.run(self.result)
assert("2 run, 1 failed" == self.result.summary())
```

~~Invoke test method~~
~~Invoke setUp first~~
~~Invoke tearDown afterward~~
Invoke tearDown even if the test method fails
~~Run multiple tests~~
~~Report collected results~~
~~Log string in WasRun~~
~~Report failed tests~~
Catch and report setUp errors
Create TestSuite from a TestCase class

All of those extra selfs are a bit ugly, but that's Python. If it were an object language, then the self would be assumed and references to global variables would require qualification. Instead, it is a scripting language with object support added (excellent object support, to be sure), so global reference is implied and referring to self is explicit.

I will leave the rest of these items to you and your new-found TDD skills.

To review, in this chapter we

- Wrote a test for a TestSuite

- Wrote part of the implementation, but without making the test work. This was a violation of "da roolz." If you spotted it at the time, take two test cases out of petty cash. I'm sure there is a simple fake implementation that would have made the test case work so we could refactor under the green bar, but I can't think what it is at the moment.

- Changed the interface of the run method so that the item and the Composite of items could work identically, then finally got the test working

- Factored out the common setup code

Chapter 24

xUnit Retrospective

If the time comes for you to implement your own testing framework, then the sequence presented in Part II of this book can serve as your guide. The details of the implementation are not nearly as important as the test cases. If you can support a set of test cases like the ones given here, then you can write tests that are isolated and can be composed, and you will be on your way to being able to develop test-first.

xUnit has been ported to more than 30 programming languages as of this writing. Your language is likely to have an implementation already. But there are a couple of reasons for implementing xUnit yourself, even if there is a version already available:

- Mastery—The spirit of xUnit is simplicity. Martin Fowler said, "Never in the annals of software engineering was so much owed by so many to so few lines of code." Some of the implementations have gotten a little complicated for my taste. Rolling your own will give you a tool over which you have a feeling of mastery.

- Exploration—When I'm faced with a new programming language, I implement xUnit. By the time I have the first eight to ten tests running, I have explored many of the facilities I will be using in daily programming.

When you begin using xUnit, you will discover a big difference between assertions that fail and other kinds of errors while running tests: assertion failures consistently take much longer to debug. Because of this, most implementations of xUnit distinguish between failures—meaning assertion failures—and errors. The GUIs present them differently, often with the errors on top.

JUnit declares a simple Test interface that both TestCase and TestSuite implement. If you want JUnit tools to be able to run your tests, then you can implement the Test interface, too.

```
public interface Test {
    public abstract int countTestCases();
    public abstract void run(TestResult result);
}
```

119

Languages with optimistic (dynamic) typing don't even have to declare their allegiance to an interface—they can just implement the operations. If you write a test scripting language, then Script can implement countTestCases() to return 1 and run to notify the TestResult on failure, and you can run your scripts along with the ordinary TestCases.

PART III

Patterns for Test-Driven Development

What follows are the "greatest hits" patterns for TDD. Some of the patterns are TDD tricks, some are design patterns, and some are refactorings. If you are familiar with one of these tricks, then the patterns here will show you how the topics play with TDD. Otherwise, there is enough material here to get you through the book examples, and to whet your appetite for the comprehensive treatments found elsewhere.

Chapter 25

Test-Driven Development Patterns

We need to answer some basic strategic questions before we can talk about the details of how to test:

- What do we mean by testing?

- When do we test?

- How do we choose what logic to test?

- How do we choose what data to test?

Test (*noun*)

How do you test your software? Write an automated test.

Test is a verb meaning "to evaluate." No software engineers release even the tiniest change without testing, except the very confident and the very sloppy. I'll assume that if you've gotten this far, you're neither. Although you may test your changes, testing changes is not the same as *having* tests. *Test* is also a noun, "a procedure leading to acceptance or rejection." Why does *test* the noun, a procedure that runs automatically, feel different from *test* the verb, such as poking a few buttons and looking at answers on the screen?

What follows is an influence diagram, à la Gerry Weinberg's Quality Software Management. An arrow between nodes means that an increase in the first node implies an increase in the second node. An arrow with a circle means that an increase in the first node implies a decrease in the second node.

What happens when the stress level rises?

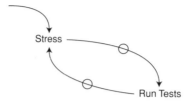

Figure 25.1 *The "no time for testing" death spiral*

This is a positive feedback loop. The more stress you feel, the less testing you will do. The less testing you do, the more errors you will make. The more errors you make, the more stress you feel. Rinse and repeat.

How do you get out of such a loop? Either introduce a new element, replace one of the elements, or change the arrows. In this case we'll replace Testing with Automated Testing.

"Did I just break something else with that change?" Figure 25.1 shows the dynamic at work. With automated tests, when I start to feel stress, I run the tests. Tests are the Programmer's Stone, transmuting fear into boredom. "No, I didn't break anything. The tests are all still green." The more stress I feel, the more I run the tests. Running the tests immediately gives me a good feeling and reduces the number of errors I make, which further reduces the stress I feel.

"We don't have time to run the tests. Just release it!" The second picture isn't guaranteed. If the stress level rises high enough, it breaks down. However, with the automated tests you have a chance to choose your level of fear.

Should you run the test after you write it, even though you know it's going to fail? No, don't bother. For example, I was working with a couple of very sharp younger programmers on implementing in-memory transactions (a very cool technique every programming language should have). The question was this: how were we going to implement rollback if we started a transaction, changed a few variables, then let the transaction be garbage collected? Simple enough to test, youngsters. Stand back and watch the master at work. Here is the test. Now how are we going to implement this?

Two hours later—hours marred with frustration because a mistake implementing such low-level features generally crashes the development environment—we rolled back to where we had started. Wrote the test. Ran it on a whim. It passed. Duh. . . . The whole point of the transaction mechanism was that variables weren't really changed until the transaction was committed. Okay, I suppose you could go ahead and run that new test if you want to.

Isolated Test

How should the running of tests affect one another? Not at all.

When I was a young programmer—long, long ago when we had to dig our own bits out of the snow and carry heavy buckets of them barefooted back to our cubicles, leaving bloody little footprints for the wolves to follow. . . . Sorry, just reminiscing. My first experience of automated tests was having a set of long-running, overnight, GUI-based tests (you know, record the keystrokes and mouse events and play them back) for a debugger I was working on. (Hi Jothy, hi John!) Every morning when I came in, there would be a neat stack of paper on my chair describing last night's test runs. (Hi Al!) On good days there would be a single sheet summarizing that nothing broke. On bad days there would be many, many sheets, one for each broken test. I began to dread days when I saw a pile of paper on my chair.

I took two lessons from this experience. First, make the tests so fast to run that I can run them myself, and run them often. That way I can catch errors before anyone else sees them, and I don't have to dread coming in in the morning. Second, I noticed after a while that a huge stack of paper didn't usually mean a huge list of problems. More often it meant that one test had broken early, leaving the system in an unpredictable state for the next test.

We tried to get around this problem by starting and stopping the system between each test, but it took too long, which taught me another lesson about seeking tests at a smaller scale than the whole application. But the main lesson I took was that tests should be able to ignore one another completely. If I had one test broken, I wanted one problem. If I had two tests broken, I wanted two problems.

One convenient implication of isolated tests is that the tests are order independent. If I want to grab a subset of tests and run them, then I can do so without worrying that a test will break now because a prerequisite test is gone.

Performance is the usual reason cited for having tests share data. A second implication of isolated tests is that you have to work, sometimes work hard, to break your problem into little orthogonal dimensions, so setting up the environment for each test is easy and quick. Isolating tests encourages you to compose solutions out of many highly cohesive, loosely coupled objects. I always heard this was a good idea, and I was happy when I achieved it, but I never knew exactly how to achieve high cohesion and loose coupling regularly until I started writing isolated tests.

Test List

What should you test? Before you begin, write a list of all the tests you know you will have to write. The first part of our approach to dealing with programming stress is never to take a step forward unless we know where our foot is going to land. When we sit down to a programming session, what is it we intend to accomplish?

One strategy for keeping track of what we're trying to accomplish is to hold it all in our heads. I tried this for several years, and found I got into a positive feedback loop. The more experience I accumulated, the more things I knew that might need to be done. The more things I knew might need to be done, the less attention I had for what I was doing. The less attention I had for what I was doing, the less I accomplished. The less I accomplished, the more things I knew that needed to be done.

Just ignoring random items on the list and programming at whim did not appear to break this cycle.

I got in the habit of writing down everything I wanted to accomplish over the next few hours on a slip of paper next to my computer. I had a similar list, but with a weekly or monthly scope, pinned on the wall. As soon as I had all that written down, I knew I wasn't going to forget something. When a new item came up, I would quickly and consciously decide whether it belonged on the "now" list or the "later" list, or whether it didn't really need to be done at all.

Applied to test-driven development, what we put on the list are the tests we want to implement. First, put on the list examples of every operation that you know you need to implement. Next, for those operations that don't already exist, put the null version of that operation on the list. Finally, list all of the refactorings that you think you will have to do in order to have clean code at the end of this session.

Instead of outlining the tests, we could just go ahead and implement them all. There are a couple of reasons writing tests en masse hasn't worked for me. First, every test you implement is a bit of inertia when you have to refactor. With automated refactoring tools (for example, you have a menu item that renames the declaration and all uses of a variable), this is less of a problem. But when you've implemented ten tests and *then* you discover that the arguments need to be in the opposite order, you are just that much less likely to go clean up. Second, if you have ten tests broken, you are a long way from the green bar. If you want to get to green quickly, you have to throw all ten tests away. If you want to get all of the tests working, then you are going to be staring at a red bar for a long time. If you are sufficiently addicted to the green bar that you can't go to the bathroom if the bar is red, then that can be an eternity.

Conservative mountain climbers have a rule that of your four hands and feet, three of them must be attached at any one time. Dynamic moves where you let go of two at once are much more dangerous. The pure form of TDD, wherein you are never more than one change away from a green bar, is like that three-out-of-four rule.

As you make the tests run, the implementation will imply new tests. Write the new tests down on the list. Likewise with refactorings.

"This is getting ugly."

"<sigh> Put it on the list. We'll get to it before we check in."

Items that are left on the list when the session is done need to be taken care of. If you are really halfway through a piece of functionality, then use the same list later. If you have discovered larger refactorings that are out of scope for the moment, then move them to the "later" list. I can't recall ever moving a test case to the "later" list. If I can think of a test that might not work, getting it to work is more important than releasing my code.

Test First

When should you write your tests? Before you write the code that is to be tested.

You won't test after. Your goal as a programmer is running functionality. However, you need a way to think about design, you need a method for scope control.

Let's consider the usual influence diagram that relates stress and testing (but not stress testing, that's different): Stress above, negatively connected to Testing below, negatively connected to Stress (see Test *(noun)* earlier in this chapter). The more stress you feel, the less likely you are to test enough. When you know you haven't tested enough, you add to your stress. Positive feedback loop. Once again, there needs to be a way to break the loop.

What if we adopted the rule that we would always test first? Then we could invert the diagram and get a virtuous cycle: Test-First above negatively connected to Stress below, negatively connected to Test-First.

When we test first, we reduce the stress, which makes us more likely to test. There are lots of other elements feeding into stress, however, so the tests must live in other virtuous cycles or they will be abandoned when stress increases enough. But the immediate payoff for testing—a design and scope control tool—suggests that we will be able to start doing it, and keep doing it even under moderate stress.

Assert First

When should you write the asserts? Try writing them first. Don't you just love self-similarity?

- Where should you start building a system? With stories you want to be able to tell about the finished system.

- Where should you start writing a bit of functionality? With the tests you want to pass with the finished code.

- Where should you start writing a test? With the asserts that will pass when it is done.

Jim Newkirk introduced me to this technique. When I test assert-first, I find it has a powerful simplifying effect. When you are writing a test, you are solving several problems at once, even if you no longer have to think about the implementation.

- Where does the functionality belong? Is it a modification of an existing method, a new method on an existing class, an existing method name implemented in a new place, or a new class?

- What should the names be called?

- How are you going to check for the right answer?

- What is the right answer?

- What other tests does this test suggest?

Pea-sized brains like mine can't possibly do a good job of solving all of these problems at once. The two problems from the list that can be easily separated from the rest are, "What is the right answer?" and "How am I going to check?"

Here's an example. Suppose we want to communicate with another system over a socket. When we're done, the socket should be closed and we should have read the string abc.

```
testCompleteTransaction() {
    ...
    assertTrue(reader.isClosed());
    assertEquals("abc", reply.contents());
}
```

Where does the reply come from? The socket, of course:

```
testCompleteTransaction() {
    ...
    Buffer reply= reader.contents();
    assertTrue(reader.isClosed());
    assertEquals("abc", reply.contents());
}
```

And the socket? We create it by connecting to a server:

```
testCompleteTransaction() {
    ...
    Socket reader= Socket("localhost", defaultPort());
    Buffer reply= reader.contents();
    assertTrue(reader.isClosed());
    assertEquals("abc", reply.contents());
}
```

But before this, we need to open a server:

```
testCompleteTransaction() {
    Server writer= Server(defaultPort(), "abc");
    Socket reader= Socket("localhost", defaultPort());
    Buffer reply= reader.contents();
    assertTrue(reader.isClosed());
    assertEquals("abc", reply.contents());
}
```

Now we may have to adjust the names based on actual usage, but we have created the outlines of the test in teeny-tiny steps, informing each decision with feedback within seconds.

Test Data

What data do you use for test-first tests? Use data that makes the tests easy to read and follow. You are writing tests to an audience. Don't scatter data values around just to be scattering data values around. If there is a difference in the data, then it should be meaningful. If there isn't a conceptual difference between 1 and 2, use 1.

Test Data isn't a license to stop short of full confidence. If your system has to handle multiple inputs, then your tests should reflect multiple inputs. However, don't have a list of ten items as the input data if a list of three items will lead you to the same design and implementation decisions.

One trick in Test Data is to try never to use the same constant to mean more than one thing. If I am testing a plus() method, it is tempting to test 2 + 2, because that is the classic example of addition, or 1 + 1, because that is so simple. What if we got the arguments reversed in the implementation? (Okay, okay, that doesn't matter in the case of plus(), but you get the idea.) If we use 2 for the first argument, for example, then we should use 3 for the second argument. (3 + 4 was a watershed test case when bringing up a new Smalltalk virtual machine back in the olden days.)

The alternative to Test Data is Realistic Data, in which you use data from the real world. Realistic Data is useful when:

- You are testing real-time systems using traces of external events gathered from the actual execution

- You are matching the output of the current system with the output of a previous system (parallel testing)

- You are refactoring a simulation and expect precisely the same answers when you are finished, particularly if floating point accuracy may be a problem

Evident Data

How do you represent the intent of the data? Include expected and actual results in the test itself, and try to make their relationship apparent. You are writing tests for a reader, not just the computer. Someone in decades to come will be asking him- or herself, "What in the heck was this joker thinking about?" You'd like to leave as many clues as possible, especially if that frustrated reader is going to be you.

Here's an example. If we convert from one currency to another, we take a 1.5 percent commission on the transaction. If the exchange rate from USD to GBP is 2:1, then if we exchange $100, we should get 50 GBP – 1.5% = 49.25 GBP. We could write this test like this:

```
Bank bank= new Bank().
bank.addRate("USD", "GBP", STANDARD_RATE);
bank.commission(STANDARD_COMMISSION);
Money result= bank.convert(new Note(100, "USD"), "GBP");
assertEquals(new Note(49.25, "GBP"), result);
```

or we could try to make the calculation obvious:

```
Bank bank= new Bank();
bank.addRate("USD", "GBP", 2);
bank.commission(0.015);
Money result= bank.convert(new Note(100, "USD"), "GBP");
assertEquals(new Note(100 / 2 * (1 - 0.015), "GBP"), result);
```

I can read this test and see the connection between the numbers used in the input and the numbers used to calculate the expected result.

One beneficial side effect of Evident Data is that it makes programming easier. Once we've written the expression in the assertion, we know what we need to program. Somehow we have to get the program to evaluate a division and a multiplication. We can even use Fake It to discover where the operations belong incrementally.

Evident Data seems to be an exception to the rule that you don't want magic numbers in your code. Within the scope of a single method, the relationship between the 5's is obvious. If I had symbolic constants that were already defined, though, I would use the symbolic form.

Chapter 26

Red Bar Patterns

These patterns are about when you write tests, where you write tests, and when you stop writing tests.

One Step Test

Which test should you pick next from the list? Pick a test that will teach you something and that you are confident you can implement.

Each test should represent one step toward your overall goal. Looking at the following Test List, then, which test should we pick next?

Plus
Minus
Times
Divide
Plus like
Equals
Equals null
Null exchange
Exchange one currency
Exchange two currencies
Cross rate

There is no right answer. What is one step for me, never having implemented these objects before, will be one-tenth of a step to you, with your vast experience. If you don't find any test on the list that represents one step, then add some new tests that would represent progress toward the items there.

When I look at a Test List, I think, "That's obvious, that's obvious, I have no idea, obvious, what was I thinking about with that one, ah, this one I can do." That last test is the test I implement next. It didn't strike me as obvious, but I'm also confident I can make it work.

A program grown from tests like this can appear to be written top-down, because you can begin with a test that represents a simple case of the entire computation. A program grown from tests can also appear to be written bottom-up, because you start with small pieces and aggregate them larger and larger.

Neither top-down nor bottom-up really describes the process helpfully. First, a vertical metaphor is a simplistic visualization of how programs change over time. *Growth* implies a kind of self-similar feedback loop in which the environment affects the program and the program affects the environment. Second, if we need to have a direction in our metaphor, then known-to-unknown is a helpful description. Known-to-unknown implies that we have some knowledge and experience on which to draw, and that we expect to learn in the course of development. Put these two together and we have programs growing from known to unknown.

Starter Test

Which test should you start with? Start by testing a variant of an operation that doesn't do anything.

The first question you have to ask with a new operation is, "Where does it belong?" Until you've answered this question, you won't know what to type for the test. In the spirit of solving one problem at a time, how can you answer just this question and no other?

If you write a realistic test first, then you will find yourself solving a bunch of problems at once:

- Where does the operation belong?

- What are the correct inputs?

- What is the correct output given those inputs?

Beginning with a realistic test will leave you too long without feedback. Red/green/refactor, red/green/refactor. You want that loop to take just minutes.

You can shorten the loop by choosing inputs and outputs that are trivially easy to discover. For example, a poster on the Extreme Programming newsgroup asked about how to write a polygon reducer test-first. The input is a mesh of polygons, and the output is a mesh of polygons that describes precisely the same surface, but with the fewest possible polygons. "How can I test-drive this problem when getting a test to work requires reading Ph.D. theses?"

Starter Test provides an answer:

- The output should be the same as the input. Some configurations of polygons are already normalized, incapable of further reduction.

- The input should be as small as possible, like a single polygon, or even an empty list of polygons.

My Starter Test looked like this:

```
Reducer r= new Reducer(new Polygon());
assertEquals(0, reducer.result().npoints);
```

Bing! The first test is running. Now for all the rest of the tests on the list. . . .

One Step Test applies to your Starter Test. Pick a Starter Test that will teach you something but that you are certain you can quickly get to work. If you are implementing an application for the nth time, then pick a test that will require an operation or two. You will be justifiably confident you can get it working. If you are implementing something hairy and complicated for the first time, then you need a little courage pill immediately.

I find that my Starter Test is often at a higher level, more like an application test, than the following tests. One example I often test-drive is a simple socket-based server. The first test looks like this:

```
StartServer
Socket= new Socket
Message= "hello"
Socket.write(message)
AssertEquals(message, socket.read)
```

The rest of the tests are written in the server alone, "Assuming we receive a string like this. . . ."

Explanation Test

How do you spread the use of automated testing? Ask for and give explanations in terms of tests.

It can be frustrating to be the only TDD on a team. Soon, you will notice fewer integration problems and defect reports in tested code, and the designs will be simpler and easier to explain. It can even happen that folks get downright enthusiastic about testing, and testing first.

Beware the enthusiasm of the newly converted. Nothing will stop the spread of TDD faster than pushing it in people's faces. If you're a manager or a leader, you can't force anyone to change the way they work.

What can you do? A simple start is to start asking for explanations in terms of test cases: "Let me see if I understand what you're saying. For example, if I have a Foo like this and a Bar like that, then the answer should be 76?" A companion technique is to start giving explanations in terms of tests: "Here's how it works now. When I have a Foo like this and a Bar like that, then the answer is 76. If I have a Foo like that and a Bar like this, though, I would like the answer to be 67."

You can do this at higher levels of abstraction. If someone is explaining a sequence diagram to you, then you can ask for permission to convert it to a more familiar notation. Then you type in a test case that contains all of the externally visible objects and messages in the diagram.

Learning Test[1]

When do you write tests for externally produced software? Before the first time you are going to use a new facility in the package.

Let's say we are going to develop something on top of the Mobile Information Device Profile library for Java. We want to store some data in the Record-Store and retrieve it. Do we just write the code and expect it to work? That's one way to develop.

An alternative is to notice that we are about to use a new method of a new class. Instead of just using it, we write a little test that verifies that the API works as expected. So, we might write:

```
RecordStore store;

public void setUp() {
    store= RecordStore.openRecordStore("testing", true);
}

public void tearDown() {
    RecordStore.deleteRecordStore("testing");
}
```

---

1. Thanks to Jim Newkirk and Laurent Bossavit for independently suggesting this pattern.

```
public void testStore() {
    int id= store.addRecord(new byte[] {5, 6}, 0, 2);
    assertEquals(2, store.getRecordSize(id));
    byte[] buffer= new byte[2];
    assertEquals(2, store.getRecord(id, buffer, 0));
    assertEquals(5, buffer[0]);
    assertEquals(6, buffer[1]);
}
```

If our understanding of the API is correct, then the test will pass first time.

Jim Newkirk reported on a project in which Learning Tests were routinely written. When new releases of the package arrived, first the tests were run (and fixed, if necessary). If the tests didn't run, then there was no sense running the application because it certainly wouldn't run. Once the tests ran, the application ran every time.

Another Test

How do you keep a technical discussion from straying off topic? When a tangential idea arises, add a test to the list and go back to the topic.

I love wandering discussions (you've read most of the book now, so you've probably reached that conclusion yourself). Keeping a conversation strictly on course is a great way to stifle brilliant ideas. You hop from here to there to there, and how did we get here? Who cares, this is cool!

Sometimes programming relies on breakthroughs. Most programming, however, is a bit more pedestrian. I have ten things to implement. I become an accomplished procrastinator about item number four. Retreating to hummingbird conversation is one of my ways of avoiding work (and maybe the fear that goes along with it).

Whole unproductive days have taught me that at times it's best to stay on track. When I'm feeling this way, I greet new ideas with respect but don't allow them to divert my attention. I write them down on the list, and then get back to what I was working on.

Regression Test

What's the first thing you do when a defect is reported? Write the smallest possible test that fails and that, once run, will be repaired.

Regression tests are tests that, with perfect foreknowledge, you would have written when coding originally. Every time you have to write a regression test, think about how you could have known to write the test in the first place.

You will also gain value by testing at the level of the whole application. Regression tests for the application give your users a chance to speak concretely to you about what is wrong and what they expect. Regression tests at the smaller scale are a way for you to improve your testing. The defect report will be about a bizarre large negative number in a report. The lesson for you is that you need to test for integer rollover when you are writing your Test List.

You may have to refactor the system before you can easily isolate the defect. The defect in this case was your system's way of telling you, "You aren't quite done designing me yet."

Break

What do you do when you feel tired or stuck? Take a break.

Take a drink, take a walk, take a nap. Wash your hands clean of your emotional commitment to the decisions you just made and the characters you typed.

Often, this amount of distance is all it will take to break loose the idea you've been lacking. You'll just be standing up when you realize, "I haven't tried it with the parameters reversed!" Take the break anyway. Give yourself a couple of minutes. The idea won't go away.

If you don't get "the idea," then review your goals for the session. Are they still realistic, or should you pick new goals? Is what you were trying to accomplish impossible? If so, what are the implications for the team?

Dave Ungar calls this his Shower Methodology. If you know what to type, then type. If you don't know what to type, then take a shower, and stay in the shower until you know what to type. Many teams would be happier, more productive, and smell a whole lot better if they took his advice. TDD is a refinement of the Ungar Shower Methodology. If you know what to type, type the Obvious Implementation. If you don't know what to type, then Fake It. If the right design still isn't clear, then Triangulate. If you *still* don't know what to type, then you can take that shower.

Figure 26.1 shows the dynamic at work in taking a Break. You're getting tired, so you're less capable of realizing that you're tired, so you keep going and get more tired.

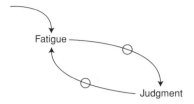

Figure 26.1 *Fatigue negatively affects Judgment, which negatively affects Fatigue*

The way out of this loop is to introduce an additional outside element.

- At the scale of hours, keep a water bottle by your keyboard so that biology provides the motivation for regular breaks.

- At the scale of a day, commitments after regular work hours can help you to stop when you need sleep before progress.

- At the scale of a week, weekend commitments help get your conscious, energy-sucking thoughts off work. (My wife swears I get my best ideas on Friday evening.)

- At the scale of a year, mandatory vacation policies help you refresh yourself completely. The French do this right—two contiguous weeks of vacation aren't enough. You spend the first week decompressing, and the second week getting ready to go back to work. Therefore, three weeks, or better four, are necessary for you to be your most effective the rest of the year.

There is a flip side to taking breaks. Sometimes when faced with a tough problem, what you need to do is press on, push through it. However, programming culture is so infected with macho spirit—"I'll ruin my health, alienate my family, and kill myself if necessary"—that I don't feel compelled to give any advice along these lines. If you find yourself caffeine-addicted and making no progress whatsoever, then perhaps you shouldn't take quite so many breaks. In the meantime, take a walk.

Do Over

What do you do when you are feeling lost? Throw away the code and start over.

You're lost. You've taken the break, rinsed your hands in the brook, sounded the Tibetan temple bell, and still you're lost. The code that was going so well an hour ago is now a mess, you can't think of how to get the next test case working, and you've thought of 20 more tests that you really should implement.

This has happened to me several times while writing this book. I would get the code a bit twisted. "But I have to finish the book. The children are starving, and the bill collectors are pounding on the door." My gut reaction would be to untwist it just enough to move on. After a pause for reflection, starting over always made more sense. The one time I pressed on regardless, I had to throw away 25 pages of manuscript because it was based on an obviously stupid programming decision.

My favorite example of doing over is a story that Tim Mackinnon told me. He was interviewing someone by the simple expedient of asking her to pair program with him for an hour. At the end of the session, they'd implemented several new test cases and done some nice refactoring. It was the end of the day, though, and they felt tired when they were done, so they discarded their work.

If you pair program, switching partners is a good way to motivate productive do-overs. You'll try to explain the complicated mess you made for a few minutes when your new partner, completely uninvested in the mistakes you've made, will gently take the keyboard and say, "I'm terribly sorry for being so dense, but what if we started like this. . . ."

Cheap Desk, Nice Chair

What physical setup should you use for TDD? Get a really nice chair, skimping on the rest of the furniture if necessary.

You can't program well if your back hurts. Yet, organizations that will spend $100,000 a month on a team won't spend $10,000 on decent chairs.

My solution is to use cheap, ugly folding tables for my computers, but buy the best chairs I can find. I have plenty of desk space, and I can easily get more, and I am fresh and ready for programming in the afternoon and the morning.

Get comfortable when you're pair programming. Clean off the desk surface enough that you can slide the keyboard back and forth. Each partner should be able to sit comfortably directly in front of the keyboard when driving. One of my favorite coaching tricks is to come up behind a pair who are hacking away and gently slide the keyboard so it is comfortably placed for the person typing.

Manfred Lange points out that careful resource allocation also applies to computer hardware. Get cheap/slow/old machines for individual e-mail and surfing, and the hottest possible machines for shared development.

Chapter 27

Testing Patterns

These patterns are more-detailed techniques for writing tests.

Child Test

How do you get a test case running that turns out to be too big? Write a smaller test case that represents the broken part of the bigger test case. Get the smaller test case running. Reintroduce the larger test case.

The red/green/refactor rhythm is so important for continuous success that when you are at risk of losing it, it is worth extra effort to maintain it. This commonly happens to me when I write a test that accidentally requires several changes in order to work. Even ten minutes with a red bar gives me the willies.

When I write a test that is too big, I first try to learn the lesson. Why was it too big? What could I have done differently that would have made it smaller? How am I feeling right now?

Metaphysical navel gazing accomplished, I delete the offending test and start over. "Well, getting these three things working at once was too much. If I had A, B, and C working, though, getting the whole thing working would be a cinch." Sometimes I really delete the test, and sometimes I just change the name to begin with an x so it won't be run. (Can I tell you a secret? Sometimes I don't even bother to delete the offending test. Shhhhh. . . . I live with two, count 'em two, broken tests for a matter of a couple of minutes while I get the child test working. I could be making a mistake when I do this. Two broken tests could easily be a holdover from my bad old test-last-if-ever days.)

Try it both ways yourself. See if you feel different, program different when you have two tests broken. Respond as appropriate.

Mock Object

How do you test an object that relies on an expensive or complicated resource? Create a fake version of the resource that answers constants.

There is at least a book's worth of material on Mock Object,[1] but this will serve as an introduction.The classic example is a database. Databases take a long time to start; they are difficult to keep clean; and if they are located on a remote server, they tie your tests to a physical location on a network. The database is also a fertile source of error in development.

The solution is not to use a real database most of the time. Most tests are written in terms of an object that acts like a database, but is really just sitting in memory.

```
public void testOrderLookup() {
    Database db= new MockDatabase();
    db.expectQuery("select order_no from Order where cust_no is 123");
    db.returnResult(new String[] {"Order 2" ,"Order 3"});
    . . .
}
```

If the MockDatabase does not get the query it expects, then it throws an exception. If the query is correct, then it returns something that looks like a result set constructed from the constant strings.

Another value of mocks, aside from performance and reliability, is readability. You can read the preceding test from one end to another. If you have a test database full of realistic data, when you see that a query should have resulted in 14 replies, you have no idea why 14 is the right answer.

If you want to use Mock Objects, you can't easily store expensive resources in global variables (even if they masquerade as Singletons). If you do, then you will have to set the global to a Mock Object, run the test, and be sure to reset the global when you are done

There have been times when I was furious with this restriction. Massimo Arnoldi and I were working on some code that relied on a set of exchange rates stored in a global variable. Each test needed different subsets of the data, and sometimes they needed different exchange rates. After a while of trying to get the global variable to work, we decided one morning (courageous design decisions come more often in the morning for me) just to pass the Exchange around wherever we needed it. We thought we would have to modify hundreds of

---

1. For example, see www.mockobjects.com.

methods. In the end, we added a parameter to ten or fifteen methods, and cleaned up other aspects of the design along the way.

Mock Objects encourage you down the path of carefully considering the visibility of every object, reducing the coupling in your designs. They add a risk to the project—what if the Mock Object doesn't behave like the real object? You can reduce this strategy by having a set of tests for the Mock Object that can also be applied to the real object when it becomes available.

Self Shunt

How do you test that one object communicates correctly with another? Have the object under test communicate with the test case instead of with the object it expects.

Suppose we wanted to dynamically update the green bar on the testing user interface. If we could connect an object to the TestResult, then it could be notified when a test ran, when it failed, when a whole suite started and finished, and so on. Whenever we were notified that a test ran, we would update the interface. Here's a test for this:

ResultListenerTest
```
def testNotification(self):
   result= TestResult()
   listener= ResultListener()
   result.addListener(listener)
   WasRun("testMethod").run(result)
   assert 1 == listener.count
```

The test needs an object to count the number of notifications:

ResultListener
```
class ResultListener:
   def __init__(self):
      self.count= 0
   def startTest(self):
      self.count= self.count + 1
```

But wait. Why do we need a separate object for the listener? We can just use the test case itself. The TestCase itself becomes a kind of Mock Object.

ResultListenerTest
```
def testNotification(self):
   self.count= 0
   result= TestResult()
   result.addListener(self)
```

```
    WasRun("testMethod").run(result)
    assert 1 == self.count
def startTest(self):
    self.count= self.count + 1
```

Tests written with Self Shunt tend to read better than tests written without it. The preceding test is a good example. The count was 0, and then it was 1. You can read the sequence right in the test. How did it get to be 1? Someone must have called startTest(). How did startTest() get called? It must happen when running the test. This is another example of symmetry—the second version of the test method has the two values for count in one place, whereas the first version has count set to 0 in one class and expected to be 1 in another.

Self Shunt may require that you use Extract Interface to get an interface to implement. You will have to decide whether extracting the interface is easier, or if testing the existing class as a black box is easier. I have noticed, however, that interfaces extracted for shunts tend to get their third and subsequent implementations soon thereafter.

As a result of using Self Shunt, you will see tests in Java that implement all sorts of bizarre interfaces. In optimistically typed languages, the test case class need only implement those operations that are actually used in the running of the test. In Java, however, you have to implement all the operations of the interface, even if most of the implementations are empty; therefore, you would want interfaces to be as narrow as possible. The implementations should either return a reasonable value or throw an exception, depending on whether you want to be notified if an unexpected operation is invoked.

Log String

How do you test that the sequence in which messages are called is correct? Keep a log in a string, and append to the string when a message is called.

The example from xUnit serves. We have a Template Method, which we expect to call setUp(), a testing method, and tearDown(), in that order. By implementing the methods to record in a string that they were called, the test reads nicely:

```
def testTemplateMethod(self):
    test= WasRun("testMethod")
    result= TestResult()
    test.run(result)
    assert("setUp testMethod tearDown " == test.log)
```

And the implementation is simple, too:

WasRun
```
def setUp(self):
    self.log= "setUp "
def testMethod(self):
    self.log= self.log + "testMethod "
def tearDown(self):
    self.log= self.log + "tearDown "
```

Log Strings are particularly useful when you are implementing Observer and you expect notifications to come in a certain order. If you expected certain notifications but you didn't care about the order, then you could keep a set of strings and use set comparison in the assertion.

Log String works well with Self Shunt. The test case implements the methods in the shunted interface by adding to the log and then returning reasonable values.

Crash Test Dummy

How do you test error code that is unlikely to be invoked? Invoke it anyway with a special object that throws an exception instead of doing real work.

Code that isn't tested doesn't work. This seems to be the safe assumption. What do you do with all those odd error conditions, then? Do you have to test them, too? Only if you want them to work.

Let's say we want to test what happens to our application when the file system is full. We could go to a lot of work to create many big files and fill the file system, or we could Fake It. Faking it doesn't sound dignified, does it? We'll *simulate* it.

Here's our Crash Test Dummy for a file:

```java
private class FullFile extends File {
    public FullFile(String path) {
        super(path);
    }
    public boolean createNewFile() throws IOException {
        throw new IOException();
    }
}
```

Now we can write our Expected Exception test:

```
public void testFileSystemError() {
   File f= new FullFile("foo");
   try {
      saveAs(f);
      fail();
   } catch (IOException e) {
   }
}
```

A Crash Test Dummy is like a Mock Object, except you don't need to mock up the whole object. Java's anonymous inner classes work well for sabotaging just the right method to simulate the error we want to exercise. You can override just the one method you want, right there in your test case, making the test case easier to read:

```
public void testFileSystemError() {
   File f= new File("foo") {
      public boolean createNewFile() throws IOException {
         throw new IOException();
      }
   };
   try {
      saveAs(f);
      fail();
   } catch (IOException e) {
   }
}
```

Broken Test

How do you leave a programming session when you're programming alone? Leave the last test broken.

Richard Gabriel taught me the trick of finishing a writing session in midsentence. When you sit back down, you look at the half-sentence and you have to figure out what you were thinking when you wrote it. Once you have the thought thread back, you finish the sentence and continue. Without the urge to finish the sentence, you can spend many minutes first sniffing around for what to work on next, then trying to remember your mental state, then finally getting back to typing.

I tried the analogous technique for my solo projects, and I really like the effect. Finish a solo session by writing a test case and running it to be sure it doesn't pass. When you come back to the code, you then have an obvious place to start. You have an obvious, concrete bookmark to help you remember what you were thinking; and making that test work should be quick work, so you'll quickly get your feet back on that victory road.

I thought it would bother me to have a test broken overnight. It doesn't, I think because I know that the program isn't finished. A broken test doesn't make the program any less finished, it just makes the status of the program manifest. The ability to pick up a thread of development quickly after weeks of hiatus is worth that little twinge of walking away from a red bar.

Clean Check-in

How do you leave a programming session when you're programming in a team? Leave all of the tests running.

Do I contradict myself? Tough.

—Bubba Whitman, Walt's stevedore brother

When you are responsible to your teammates, the picture changes completely. When you start programming on a team project, you don't know in detail what has happened to the code since you saw it last. You need to start from a place of confidence and certainty. Therefore, always make sure that all of the tests are running before you check in your code. (It's a bit like how each test case leaves the world in a known good state, if you are prone to computer metaphors for human behavior, which I'm not, usually.)

The test suite you run when you check in may be more extensive than the one you are running every minute during development. (Don't give up on running the whole suite all the time until it is slow enough to be annoying.) You will occasionally find a test broken in the integration suite when you try to check in. What to do?

The simplest rule is to just throw away your work and start over. The broken test is pretty strong evidence that you didn't know enough to program what you just programmed. If the team adopted this rule, then there would be a tendency for folks to check in more often because the first person to check in wouldn't risk losing any work. Checking in more often is probably a good thing.

A slightly more libertine approach gives you a chance to fix the defect and try again. To keep from dominating the integration resources, you should probably give up after a few minutes and start over. It goes without saying, but I'll say it anyway, that commenting out tests to make the suite pass is strictly verboten, and grounds for some serious beer purchasing at that Friday's late afternoon offsite planning meeting.

Chapter 28

Green Bar Patterns

Once you have a broken test, you need to fix it. If you treat a red bar as a condition to be fixed as quickly as possible, then you will discover that you can get to green quickly. Use these patterns to make the code pass (even if the result isn't something you want to live with for even an hour).

Fake It ('Til You Make It)

What is your first implementation once you have a broken test? Return a constant. Once you have the test running, gradually transform the constant into an expression using variables.

A simple example occurred in our implementation of xUnit:

```
return "1 run, 0 failed"
```

became:

```
return "%d run, 0 failed" % self.runCount
```

became:

```
return "%d run, %d failed" % (self.runCount , self failureCount)
```

Fake It is a bit like driving a piton above your head when you are climbing a rock. You haven't really gotten there yet (the test is there but the code structure is wrong). But when you do get there, you know you will be safe (the test will still run).

Fake It really rubs some people the wrong way. Why would you do something that you know you will have to rip out? Because having something running is better than not having something running, especially if you have the tests to prove it. Peter Hansen submitted this story:

> Something happened just yesterday where, as two newbies to TDD, my partner and I aggressively stuck to the letter of the law and committed sins to get a test working quickly. In the process, we realized we had not properly implemented the test so we went back and fixed that, then made the code work again. The first working code ended up not being anywhere in sight by the time it worked again and we sort of looked at each other and said, "Huh . . . would you look at that!" because that approach had taught us something we didn't know.

How could a fake implementation have taught them their test was written wrong? I don't know, but I'll bet they were glad they didn't invest in the real solution to find out.

There are a couple of effects that make Fake It powerful.

- Psychological—Having a green bar feels completely different from having a red bar. When the bar is green, you know where you stand. You can refactor from there with confidence.

- Scope control—Programmers are good at imagining all sorts of future problems. Starting with one concrete example and generalizing from there prevents you from prematurely confusing yourself with extraneous concerns. You can do a better job of solving the immediate problem because you are focused. When you go to implement the next test case, you can focus on that one, too, knowing that the previous test is guaranteed to work.

Does Fake It violate the rule that says you don't write any code that isn't needed? I don't think so, because in the refactoring step you are eliminating duplication of data between the test case and the code. When I write[1]:

```
assertEquals(new MyDate("28.2.02"), new MyDate("1.3.02").yesterday());
```

MyDate
```
public MyDate yesterday() {
    return new MyDate("28.2.02");
}
```

there is duplication between the test and the code. I can shift it around by writing:

MyDate
```
public MyDate yesterday() {
    return new MyDate(new MyDate("31.3.02").days()-1);
}
```

---

1. Thanks to Dierk König for the example.

But there is still duplication. However, I can eliminate the data duplication (because this equals MyDate("31.1.02") for the purposes of my test) by writing:

MyDate
```
public MyDate yesterday() {
    return new MyDate(this.days()-1);
}
```

Not everyone is convinced by this bit of sophistry, which is why you can use Triangulation, at least until you are tired of it, and start using Fake It or even Obvious Implementation.

When I use Fake It, I'm reminded of long car trips with kids in the back. I write the first test, I make it work some ugly way, and then, "Don't make me stop this car and write another test. If I have to pull over, you'll be sorry."

"Okay, okay, Dad. I'll clean the code up. You don't have to get all huffy."

Triangulate

How do you most conservatively drive abstraction with tests? Abstract only when you have two or more examples.

Here's such a situation. Suppose we want to write a function that will return the sum of two integers. We write:

```
public void testSum() {
    assertEquals(4, plus(3, 1));
}

private int plus(int augend, int addend) {
    return 4;
}
```

If we are triangulating to the right design, we have to write:

```
public void testSum() {
    assertEquals(4, plus(3, 1));
    assertEquals(7, plus(3,4));
}
```

When we have the second example, we can abstract the implementation of plus():

```
private int plus(int augend, int addend) {
    return augend + addend;
}
```

Triangulation is attractive because the rules for it seem so clear. The rules for Fake It, which rely on our sense of duplication between the test case and the fake implementation to drive abstraction, seem a bit vague and subject to interpretation. Although they seem simple, the rules for Triangulation create an infinite loop. Once we have the two assertions and we have abstracted the correct implementation for plus, we can delete one of the assertions on the grounds that it is completely redundant with the other. If we do that, however, we can simplify the implementation of plus() to return just a constant, which requires us to add an assertion.

I only use Triangulation when I'm really, really unsure about the correct abstraction for the calculation. Otherwise I rely on either Obvious Implementation or Fake It.

Obvious Implementation

How do you implement simple operations? Just implement them.

Fake It and Triangulation are teensy-weensy tiny steps. Sometimes you are sure you know how to implement an operation. Go ahead. For example, would I really use Fake It to implement something as simple as plus()? Not usually. I would just type in the Obvious Implementation. If I noticed I was getting surprised by red bars, then I would go to smaller steps.

There's no particular virtue in the halfway nature of Fake It and Triangulation. If you know what to type, and you can do it quickly, then do it. However, by using only Obvious Implementation, you are demanding perfection of yourself.[2] Psychologically, this can be a devastating move. What if what you write isn't really the simplest change that could get the test to pass? What if your partner shows you an even simpler one? You're a failure! Your world crumbles around you! You die. You freeze up.

Solving "clean code" at the same time that you solve "that works" can be too much to do at once. As soon as it is, go back to solving "that works," and then "clean code" at leisure.

Keep track of how often you are surprised by red bars using Obvious Implementation. I'll get stuck in these cycles where I'll type in an Obvious Implementation, but it won't work. But now I'm sure I know what I should type, so I type

---

2. Thanks to Laurent Bossavit for this discussion.

that. It doesn't work. So now. . . . This especially happens with off-by-one errors and positive/negative errors.

You want to maintain that red/green/refactor rhythm. Obvious Implementation is second gear. Be prepared to downshift if your brain starts writing checks your fingers can't cash.

One to Many

How do you implement an operation that works with collections of objects? Implement it without the collections first, then make it work with collections.

For example, suppose we are writing a function to sum an array of numbers. We can start with one:

```
public void testSum() {
    assertEquals(5, sum(5));
}

private int sum(int value) {
    return value;
}
```

(I am implementing sum() in the TestCase class to avoid writing a new class just for one method.)

We want to test sum(new int[] {5, 7}) next. First we add a parameter to sum(), taking an array of values:

```
public void testSum() {
    assertEquals(5, sum(5, new int[] {5}));
}

private int sum(int value, int[] values) {
    return value;
}
```

We can look at this step as an example of Isolate Change. Once we add the parameter in the test case, we are free to change the implementation without affecting the test case.

Now we can use the collection instead of the single value:

```
private int sum(int value, int[] values) {
    int sum= 0;
    for (int i= 0; i<values.length; i++)
        sum += values[i];
    return sum;
}
```

Next we can delete the unused single parameter:

```
public void testSum() {
    assertEquals(5, sum(new int[] {5}));
}

private int sum(int[] values) {
    int sum= 0;
    for (int i= 0; i<values.length; i++)
        sum += values[i];
    return sum;
}
```

The preceding step is also an example of Isolate Change, where we change the code so we can change the test cases without affecting the code. Now we can enrich the test case as planned:

```
public void testSum() {
    assertEquals(12, sum(new int[] {5, 7}));
}
```

Chapter 29

xUnit Patterns

These are patterns for using one of the xUnit family of testing frameworks.

Assertion

How do you check that tests worked correctly? Write boolean expressions that automate your judgment about whether the code worked.

If we are going to make the tests fully automated, then every bit of human judgment has to be taken out of the evaluation of the results. We need to push a button and make all of the decisions necessary to verify the correct working of the code that the computer runs. This suggests the following.

- The decisions have to be boolean—*True* generally means everything is okay, and *false* means something unexpected happened.

- The state of the booleans have to be checked by computer, by calling some variant of an assert() method

I've seen assertions like assertTrue(rectangle.area() != 0). You could return anything not null and satisfy this test, so it isn't very useful. Be specific. If the area should be 50, then say that it should be 50: assertTrue(rectangle.area() == 50). Many xUnit implementations have a special assertion for testing equality. Testing for equality is common, and if you know you are testing equality, you can write an informative error message. The expected value generally goes first, so in JUnit we would write this as assertEquals(50, rectangle.area()).

Thinking about objects as black boxes is hard. If I have a Contract with a Status that can be an instance of either Offered or Running, I might feel like writing a test based on my expected implementation:

```
Contract contract= new Contract(); // Offered status by default
contract.begin(); // Changes status to Running
assertEquals(Running.class, contract.status.class);
```

This test is too dependent on the current implementation of status. The test should pass even if the representation of status changed to a boolean. Perhaps once the status changes to Running, it is possible to ask for the actual start date.

```
assertEquals(. . ., contract.startDate()); // Throws an exception if the status is Offered
```

I'm aware that I am swimming against the tide in insisting that all tests be written using only public protocol. There is even a package that extends JUnit called JXUnit, which allows testing the value of variables, even those declared private.

Wishing for white box testing is not a testing problem, it is a design problem. Anytime I want to use a variable as a way of checking to see whether code ran correctly or not, I have an opportunity to improve the design. If I give in to my fear and just check the variable, then I lose that opportunity. That said, if the design idea doesn't come, it doesn't come. I'll check the variable, shed a tear, make a note to come back on one of my smarter days, and move on.

The original SUnit (the first, Smalltalk, version of the testing framework) had simple assertions. If one broke, then a debugger popped up, you fixed the code, and away you went. Because the IDEs for Java aren't as sophisticated, and because building Java-based software often happens in a batch environment, it makes sense to add information about the assertion that will be printed if it ever fails.

In JUnit, this takes the form of an optional first parameter.[1] If you write assertTrue("Should be true", false) when the test is run, you will see an error message something like "Assertion failed: Should be true". This is often enough information to send you straight to the source of the error in the code. Some teams adopt the convention that all assertions must be accompanied by an informative error message. Try it both ways and see if the investment in the error messages pays off for you.

Fixture

How do you create common objects needed by several tests? Convert the local variables in the tests into instance variables. Override setUp() and initialize those variables.

If we want to remove duplication from our model code, do we want to remove it from our test code also? Maybe.

---

1. Optional parameters are supposed to come at the end, but for readability of the tests it helps to have the explanatory string at the beginning.

Here's the problem: Often you write more code setting objects up in an interesting state than you write manipulating them and checking results. The code for setting up the objects is the same for several tests (these objects are the test's fixture, also known as scaffolding.) This duplication is bad, for the following reasons.

- It takes a while to write, even to copy and paste, and we'd like test writing to be fast.

- If we need to change an interface by hand, then we have to change it in several tests (exactly what we would expect of duplication).

The same duplication, however, is also good. Tests written with the setup code right there with the assertions are readable from top to bottom. If we factored the setup code into a separate method, then we would have to remember that the method was called, and remember what the objects looked like, before we could write the rest of the test.

xUnit supports both styles of test writing. You can write the test-fixture-creating code with the test, if you expect readers not to be able to remember the fixture objects easily. However, you can also move common test-fixture-creating code into a method called setUp(). In it, set instance variables to the objects that will be used in the test.

Here is an example too simple to motivate the value of factoring out common setup code, but short enough to fit in this book. We could write:

EmptyRectangleTest

```
public void testEmpty() {
    Rectangle empty= new Rectangle(0,0,0,0);
    assertTrue(empty.isEmpty());
}

public void testWidth() {
    Rectangle empty= new Rectangle(0,0,0,0);
    assertEquals(0.0, empty.getWidth(), 0.0);
}
```

(This also demonstrates the floating point version of assertEquals(), which requires a tolerance.) We could get rid of the duplication by writing:

EmptyRectangleTest

```
private Rectangle empty;

public void setUp() {
    empty= new Rectangle(0,0,0,0);
}
```

```
public void testEmpty() {
    assertTrue(empty.isEmpty());
}

public void testWidth() {
    assertEquals(0.0, empty.getWidth(), 0.0);
}
```

We have extracted the common code as a method, one that the framework is guaranteed to call before our test method is called. The test methods are simpler, but we have to remember what is in setUp() before we can understand them.

Which style should you use? Try them both. I nearly always factor out common setup code, but I have a strong memory for detail. Readers of my tests sometimes complain that there is too much to remember, so maybe I should factor out less.

The relationship of subclasses of TestCase and instances of those subclasses is one of the most confusing parts of xUnit. Each new kind of fixture should be a new subclass of TestCase. Each new fixture is created in an instance of that subclass, used once, and then discarded.

In the preceding example, if we wanted to write tests for a nonempty Rectangle, then we would create a new class, perhaps NormalRectangleTest, and initialize a different variable to a different rectangle in setUp(). In general, if I find myself wanting a slightly different fixture, then I start a new subclass of TestCase.

This implies that there is no simple relationship between test classes and model classes. Sometimes one fixture serves to test several classes (although this is rare). Sometimes two or three fixtures are needed for a single model class. In practice, you usually end up with roughly the same number of test classes as model classes, but not because for each and every model class you write one and only one test class.

External Fixture

How do you release external resources in the fixture? Override tearDown() and release the resources.

Remember that the goal of each test is to leave the world in exactly the same state as before it ran. For example, if you open a file during a test, you need to be sure to close it before the test completes. You could write:

```
testMethod(self):
    file= File("foobar").open()
```

```
try:
    ...run the test...
finally:
    file.close()
```

If the file were used in several tests, then you could make it part of the common fixture:

```
setUp(self):
    self.file= File("foobar").open()
testMethod(self):
    try:
        ...run the test...
    finally:
        self.file.close()
```

First, there is that pesky duplication of the finally clause telling us that we are missing something in the design. Second, this method is error prone because it is easy to forget the finally clause, or to forget to close the file altogether. Finally, there are three lines of noise in the test—try, finally, and the close itself, which is not central to the running of the test.

xUnit guarantees that a method called tearDown() will be run after the test method. TearDown() will be called regardless of what happens in the test method (although if setUp() fails, tearDown() won't be called). We can transform the preceding test into:

```
setUp(self):
    self.file= File("foobar").open()
testMethod(self):
    ...run the test...
tearDown(self):
    self.file.close()
```

Test Method

How do you represent a single test case? As a method whose name begins with "test."

You are going to have hundreds, later thousands, of tests in your system. How are you going to keep track of them all?

Object programming languages have three levels of hierarchy for organization:

- Module ("package" in Java)

- Class

- Method

If we are writing tests as ordinary source code, then we need to find a way to fit into this structure. If we are using classes to represent fixtures, then the natural home for tests is as methods. All of the tests that share a single fixture will be methods in the same class. Tests that require a different fixture will be in a different class.

By convention, the name of the method begins with "test." Tools can look for this pattern to automatically create suites of tests given a class. The remainder of the method name should suggest to a future clueless reader why this test was written. JUnit, for example has a test called "testAssertPosInfinityNotEqualsNegInfinity". I can't remember writing this test, but from the name I assume that at some point JUnit's assertion code for floating point numbers didn't distinguish between positive and negative infinity. From the test I can quickly find the code in JUnit that handles floating point comparison and see how we handled it. (It's kind of ugly—there's a special conditional to handle infinity.)

Test methods should be easy to read, pretty much straightline code. If a test method is getting long and complicated, then you need to play "Baby Steps." The goal of the game is to write the smallest test method that represents real progress toward your end goal. Three lines appears to be about the minimum, without deliberate obfuscation (and remember, you are writing these tests for people, not just the computer or yourself).

Patrick Logan contributed an idea I'm going to experiment with, also described by McConnell[2] and Caine and Gordon,[3]

> For some reason I've been working with "outlines" in practically everything I do lately. Testing is no different. When I write tests, I first create a short outline of the tests I want to write, for example. . .

```
/* Adding to tuple spaces. */
/* Taking from tuple spaces. */
/* Reading from tuple space. */
```

> These are place holders until I add specific tests under each category. When I add tests, I add another level of comments to the outline. . .

```
/* Adding to tuple spaces. */
/* Taking from tuple spaces. */
/** Taking a non-existent tuple. **/
/** Taking an existing tuple. **/
/** Taking multiple tuples. **/
/* Reading from tuple space. */
```

2. McConnell, Steve. 1993. *Code Complete*, chapter 4. Seattle, Washington: Microsoft Press. ISBN 1556154844.

3. Caine, S. H., and Gordon, E. K. 1975. "PDL: A Tool for Software Design," *AFIPS Proceedings of the 1975 National Computer Conference.*

I usually only have two or three levels to the outline. I can't think of when I had more. But the outline essentially becomes documentation of the contract for the class being tested. The examples here are abbreviated, but they would be more specific in a contract-like language. (I don't use any kind of add-on to Java for Eiffel-like automation.)

Immediately under the lowest level of the outline is the test case code.

Exception Test

How do you test for expected exceptions? Catch expected exceptions and ignore them, failing only if the exception isn't thrown.

Let's say we're writing some code to look up a value. If the value isn't found, then we want to throw an exception. Testing the lookup is easy enough:

```
public void testRate() {
    exchange.addRate("USD", "GBP", 2);
    int rate= exchange.findRate("USD", "GBP");
    assertEquals(2, rate);
}
```

Testing the exception may not be so obvious. Here's how we do it:

```
public void testMissingRate() {
    try {
        exchange.findRate("USD", "GBP");
        fail();
    } catch (IllegalArgumentException expected) {
    }
}
```

If findRate() doesn't throw an exception, we will call fail(), an xUnit method which reports that the test failed. Notice that we are careful only to catch the particular exception we expect, so we will also be notified if the wrong kind of exception is thrown (including assertion failures).

All Tests

How do you run all tests together? Make a suite of all the suites—one for each package, and one aggregating the package tests for the whole application.

Suppose you add a TestCase subclass to a package and you add a test method to that class. The next time all of the tests run, that test method should run, too. (There's that test-driven stuff—the preceding is the outline for a test that I would probably just go and implement if I weren't busy writing a book.) Because this isn't supported in most xUnit implementations or IDEs, each package should declare a class AllTests that implements a static method suite() that returns a TestSuite. Here is AllTests for the money example:

```
public class AllTests {
    public static void main(String[] args) {
        junit.swingui.TestRunner.run(AllTests.class);
    }

    public static Test suite() {
        TestSuite result= new TestSuite("TFD tests");
        result.addTestSuite(MoneyTest.class);
        result.addTestSuite(ExchangeTest.class);
        result.addTestSuite(IdentityRateTest.class);
        return result;
    }
}
```

You can also give AllTests a main() method so that the class can be run directly from the IDE or a command line.

Chapter 30

Design Patterns

One of the primary insights of patterns is that although it may seem as though we solve completely different problems all the time, most of the problems we solve are generated by the tools we use, not by the external problem at hand.[1] Because of this, we can expect to find (and actually do find) common problems with common solutions even in the midst of an incredible diversity of external problem solving contexts.

Applying objects to organizing computation is one of the best examples of common internally generated subproblems being solved in common, predictable ways. The enormous success of design patterns is a testimonial to the commonality seen by object programmers.[2] The success of the book *Design Patterns*, however, has stifled any diversity in expressing these patterns. The book seems to have a subtle bias toward design as a phase. It certainly makes no nod toward refactoring as a design activity. Design in TDD requires a slightly different look at design patterns.

The design patterns covered here are not intended to be comprehensive. They are just enough design to get us through the examples. Here they are in summary.

- Command—Represent the invocation of a computation as an object, not just as a message.

- Value Object—Avoid aliasing problems by making objects whose values never change once created.

---

1. Alexander, Christopher. 1970. *Notes on the Synthesis of Form*. Cambridge, MA: Harvard University Press. ISBN: 0674627512.
2. Gamma, Erich; Helm, Richard; Johnson, Ralph; Vlissides, John. 1995. *Design Patterns: Elements of Reusable Object Oriented Software*. Boston: Addison-Wesley. ISBN: 0201633612.

- Null Object—Represent the base case of a computation by an object.

- Template Method—Represent invariant sequences of computation with an abstract method intended to be specialized through inheritance.

- Pluggable Object—Represent variation by invoking another object with two or more implementations.

- Pluggable Selector—Avoid gratuitous subclasses by dynamically invoking different methods for different instances.

- Factory Method—Create an object by calling a method instead of a constructor.

- Imposter—Introduce variation by introducing a new implementation of existing protocol.

- Composite—Represent the composition of the behavior of a list of objects with an object.

- Collecting Parameter—Pass around a parameter to be used to aggregate the results of computation in many different objects.

The design patterns cluster based on where they are used in TDD, as shown in Table 29.1.

Table 30.1 *Use of Design Patterns in Test-Driven Development*

Pattern	Test Writing	Refactoring
Command	X	
Value Object	X	
Null Object		X
Template Method		X
Pluggable Object		X
Pluggable Selector		X
Factory Method	X	X
Imposter	X	X
Composite	X	X
Collecting Parameter	X	X

Command

What do you do when you need the invocation of a computation to be more complicated than a simple method call? Make an object for the computation and invoke it.

Sending messages is wonderful. Programming languages make sending messages syntactically easy; and programming environments make manipulating messages easy (for example, refactorings to rename a message automatically). However, sometimes just sending a message isn't enough.

For example, suppose we wanted to log the fact that a message got sent. We could add language features (wrapper methods) to do this, but logging is rare enough, and the value of simple languages is high enough, that we'd rather not do that. Or suppose we wanted to invoke a computation, but later. We could start a thread, immediately suspend it, and restart it later, but then we'd have all the joys of concurrency to deal with.

Complicated invocations of computation require expensive mechanisms. But most of the time we don't need all the complexity, and we'd rather not pay the cost. When we need invocation to be just a little more concrete and manipulable than a message, objects give us the answer. Make an object representing the invocation. Seed it with all the parameters the computation will need. When we're ready to invoke it, use generic protocol, like run().

The Java interface Runnable is an excellent example of this:

Runnable
```
interface Runnable
  public abstract void run();
```

In the implementation of run(), you can do anything you'd like. Unfortunately, Java has no syntactically lightweight way to create and invoke Runnables, so they aren't used as much as the equivalent in other languages—blocks or lambda in Smalltalk/Ruby or LISP.

Value Object

How do you design objects that will be widely shared, but for whom identity is unimportant? Set their state when they are created and never change it. Operations on the object always return a new object.

Objects are wonderful. I can say that here, can't I? Objects are a great way to organize logic for later understanding and growth. However, there is one little problem (okay, more than one, but this one will do for now).

Suppose I (an object) have a Rectangle. I compute some value based on the Rectangle, like its area. Later, someone politely asks me for my Rectangle, and I, not wanting to appear uncooperative, give it to them. Moments later, lo and behold, the Rectangle has been changed behind my back. The area I computed earlier is out of date, and there is no way for me to know.

This is the classic aliasing problem. If two objects share a reference to a third, and if one object changes the shared object, then the other object better not rely on the state of the shared object.

There are several ways out of the aliasing problem. One solution is never to give out the objects that you rely on, but instead always make copies. This can get expensive in time and space, and ignores those times when you want to share changes to a shared object. Another solution is Observer, where you explicit register with objects on which you rely and expect to be notified when they change. Observer can make control flows difficult to follow, and the logic for setting up and removing the dependencies gets ugly.

Another solution is to treat the object as less than an object. Objects have a state that change over time. We can, if we choose, eliminate "that change over time." If I have an object and I know it won't change, then I can pass around references to it all I want, knowing that aliasing won't be a problem. There can be no hidden changes to a shared object if there are no changes.

I remember puzzling over integers when I was first learning Smalltalk. If I change bit 2 to a 1, why don't all 2's become 6's?

```
a := 2.
b := a.
a := a bitAt: 2 put: 1.
a => 6
b => 2
```

Integers are really values masquerading as objects. In Smalltalk this is literally true of small integers, and simulated in the case of integers that don't fit in a single machine word. When I set that bit, what I get back is a new object with the bit set, not the old one with the bit changed.

When implementing a Value Object, every operation has to return a fresh object, leaving the original unchanged. Users have to be aware that they are using a Value Object and store the result (as in the preceding above.) All of these object allocations can create performance problems, which should be handled like all performance problems, when you have realistic data sets, realistic usage patterns, profiling data, and complaints about performance.

I have a tendency to use Value Object whenever I have a situation that looks like algebra—geometric shapes being intersected and unioned, unit values where units are carried around with a number, symbolic arithmetic. Any time Value Object makes the least sense I try it, because it makes reading and debugging so much easier.

All Value Objects have to implement equality (and in many languages by implication they have to implement hashing). If I have this contract and that contract and they aren't the same object, then they are different, not equal. However, if I have this five francs and that five francs, it doesn't matter if they are the same five francs; five francs are five francs, and they should be equal.

Null Object

How do you represent special cases using objects? Create an object representing the special case. Give it the same protocol as the regular objects.

inspired by java.io.File
```
public boolean setReadOnly() {
    SecurityManager guard = System.getSecurityManager();
    if (guard != null) {
        guard.canWrite(path);
    }
    return fileSystem.setReadOnly(this);
}
```

There are 18 checks for guard != null in java.io.File. Although I appreciate their diligence in making files safe for the world, I'm also a bit nervous. Are they careful to always check for a null as the result of getSecurityManager()?

The alternative is to create a new class, LaxSecurity, which doesn't throw exceptions ever:

LaxSecurity
```
public void canWrite(String path) {
}
```

If someone asks for a SecurityManager and there isn't one available, then we send back a LaxSecurity instead:

SecurityManager
```
public static SecurityManager getSecurityManager() {
    return security == null ? new LaxSecurity() : security;
}
```

Now we don't have to worry about someone forgetting to check for null. The original code cleans up considerably:

File

```java
public boolean setReadOnly() {
    SecurityManager security = System.getSecurityManager();
    security.canWrite(path);
    return fileSystem.setReadOnly(this);
}
```

Erich Gamma and I once got in an argument at an OOPSLA tutorial about whether a Null Object was appropriate somewhere in JHotDraw. I was ahead on points when Erich calculated the cost of introducing the Null Object as ten lines of code, for which we would get to eliminate one conditional. I hate those late round TKOs (technical knock-outs). (We also got extremely bad marks from the audience for not being organized. Apparently they weren't aware that having productive design discussions is a difficult but learnable skill.)

Template Method

How do you represent the invariant sequence of a computation while providing for future refinement? Write a method that is implemented entirely in terms of other methods.

Programming is full of classic sequences:

- input/process/output

- Send message/receive reply

- Read command/return result

We would like to be able to clearly communicate the universality of these sequences, and at the same time provide for variation in the implementation of the steps.

In inheritance, object languages provide a simple, if limited, mechanism for communicating universal sequences. A superclass can contain a method written entirely in terms of other methods, and subclasses can implement those methods in different ways. For example, JUnit implements the basic sequence of running a test as:

TestCase

```java
public void runBare() throws Throwable {
    setUp();
    try {
        runTest();
```

```
    }
    finally {
        tearDown();
    }
}
```

Subclasses can implement setUp(), runTest(), and tearDown() however they want.

One question when writing a Template Method is whether to write a default implementation of the submethods. In TestCase.runBare(), all three submethods have default implementations.

- setUp() and tearDown() are no-ops.

- runTest() dynamically finds and invokes a testing method based on the name of the test case.

If the computation makes no sense without a substep being filled in, then note this in whatever way your programming language provides.

- In Java, declare the submethod abstract.

- In Smalltalk, implement the method by throwing a SubclassResponsibility error.

Template methods are best found through experience instead of designed that way from the beginning. Whenever I say to myself, "Ah, this is the sequence and here are the details," I always find myself inlining the detail methods later and re-extracting the truly variant parts.

When you find two variants of a sequence in two subclasses, you need to gradually move them closer together. Once you've extracted the parts that are different from other methods, what you are left with is the Template Method. Then you can move the Template Method to the superclass and eliminate the duplication.

Pluggable Object

How do you express variation? The simplest way is with explicit conditionals:

```
if (circle) then {
. . . circley stuff. . .
} else {
. . . non circley stuff
}
```

You will quickly find that such explicit decision making begins to spread. If you represent the distinction between circles and noncircles as an explicit conditional in one place, then the conditional is likely to spread.

Because the second imperative of TDD is the elimination of duplication, you must nip the plague of explicit conditionals in the bud. The second time you see a conditional, it is time to pull out the most basic of object design moves, the Pluggable Object.

The Pluggable Objects revealed by simply eliminating duplication are sometimes counterintuitive. Erich Gamma and I found this, one of my favorite examples of an unpredictable Pluggable Object. When writing a graphics editor, selection is actually a bit complicated. If you're over a figure when you press the mouse button, then subsequent moves of the mouse move that figure and releasing the mouse button leaves the figure selected. If you're not over a figure, then you are selecting a group of figures, and subsequent moves of the mouse typically resize a rectangle used to select several figures. Releasing the mouse button causes the figures inside the rectangle to be selected. The initial code looks something like this:

SelectionTool
```
Figure selected;
public void mouseDown() {
    selected= findFigure();
    if (selected != null)
        select(selected);
}
public void mouseMove() {
    if (selected != null)
        move(selected);
    else
        moveSelectionRectangle();
}
public void mouseUp() {
    if (selected == null)
        selectAll();
}
```

There's that ugly duplicated conditional (I told you they spread like a disease). The answer in this case is to create a Pluggable Object, a SelectionMode, with two implementations, SingleSelection and MultipleSelection.

SelectionTool
```
SelectionMode mode;
public void mouseDown() {
    selected= findFigure();
    if (selected != null)
        mode= SingleSelection(selected);
    else
        mode= MultipleSelection();
```

```
}
public void mouseMove() {
   mode.mouseMove();
}
public void mouseUp() {
   mode.mouseUp();
}
```

In languages with explicit interfaces, you will have to implement an interface along with the two (or more) Pluggable Objects.

Pluggable Selector[3]

How do you invoke different behavior for different instances? Store the name of a method, and dynamically invoke the method.

What do you do when you have ten subclasses of a class, each implementing only one method? Subclassing is a heavyweight mechanism for capturing such a small amount of variation.

```
abstract class Report {
   abstract void print();
}

class HTMLReport extends Report {
   void print() { ...
   }
}

class XMLReport extends Report {
   void print() { ...
   }
}
```

One alternative is to have a single class with a switch statement. Depending on the value of a field, you invoke different methods. However, the name of the method appears in three places:

- The creation of the instance

- The switch statement

- The method itself

---

3. For more details, see Beck, K. 1997. *The Smalltalk Best Practice Patterns*, pp. 70–73. Englewood-Cliffs, NJ: Prentice-Hall. ISBN 013476904X. It's bad form to reference your own works, but as noted philosopher Phyllis Diller once said, "Of course I laugh at my own jokes. You can't trust strangers."

```
abstract class Report {
   String printMessage;

   Report(String printMessage) {
      this.printMessage= printMessage;
   }

   void print() {
      switch (printMessage) {
         case "printHTML" :
            printHTML();
            break;
         case "printXML" :
            printXML():
            break;
      }
   };

   void printHTML() {
   }

   void printXML() {
   }
}
```

Every time you add a new kind of printing, you have to be sure to add the print-ing method and change the switch statement.

The Pluggable Selector solution is to dynamically invoke the method using reflection:

```
void print() {
   Method runMethod= getClass().getMethod(printMessage, null);
   runMethod.invoke(this, new Class[0]);
}
```

Now there is still an ugly dependency between creators of reports and the names of the print methods, but at least you don't have the case statement in there, too.

Pluggable Selector can definitely be overused. The biggest problem with it is tracing code to see whether a method is invoked. Use Pluggable Selector only when you are cleaning up a fairly straightforward situation in which each of a bunch of subclasses has only one method.

Factory Method

How do you create an object when you want flexibility in creating new objects? Create the object in a method instead of using a constructor.

Constructors are expressive. You can see that you are definitely creating an object when you use one. However, constructors, particularly in Java, lack expressiveness and flexibility.

One axis of flexibility that we wanted in our money example was to be able to return an object of a different class when we created an object. We had tests like:

```
public void testMultiplication() {
   Dollar five= new Dollar(5);
   assertEquals(new Dollar(10), five.times(2));
   assertEquals(new Dollar(15), five.times(3));
}
```

We wanted to introduce the Money class, but we couldn't as long as we were locked into creating an instance of Dollar. By introducing a level of indirection, through a method, we gained the flexibility of returning an instance of a different class without changing the test:

```
public void testMultiplication() {
  Dollar five = Money.dollar(5);
   assertEquals(new Dollar(10), five.times(2));
   assertEquals(new Dollar(15), five.times(3));
}
```

Money
```
static Dollar dollar(int amount) {
   return new Dollar(amount);
}
```

This method is called a Factory Method, because it makes objects.

The downside of using Factory Method is precisely its indirection. You have to remember that the method is really creating an object, even though it doesn't look like a constructor. Use Factory Method only when you need the flexibility it creates. Otherwise, constructors work just fine for creating objects.

Imposter

How do you introduce a new variation into a computation? Introduce a new object with the same protocol as an existing object but a different implementation.

Introducing variation in a procedural program involves adding conditional logic. As we saw with Pluggable Object, such logic tends to proliferate, and a healthy dose of polymorphic messages are required to cure the duplication.

Suppose you have a structure in place already. There's an object already. Now you need the system to do something different. If there's an obvious place to insert an *if* statement and you're not duplicating logic from elsewhere, then go ahead. Often, however, the variation would obviously require changes to several methods.

This moment of decision comes up in two ways in TDD. Sometimes you are writing a test case and you need to represent a new scenario. None of the existing objects expresses what you want to express. Suppose we are testing a graphics editor and we already have rectangles drawing correctly:

```
testRectangle() {
    Drawing d= new Drawing();
    d.addFigure(new RectangleFigure(0, 10, 50, 100));
    RecordingMedium brush= new RecordingMedium();
    d.display(brush);
    assertEquals("rectangle 0 10 50 100\n", brush.log());
}
```

Now we want to display ovals. In this case, the Imposter is easy to spot—replace a RectangleFigure with an OvalFigure.

```
testOval() {
    Drawing d= new Drawing();
    d.addFigure(new OvalFigure(0, 10, 50, 100));
    RecordingMedium brush= new RecordingMedium();
    d.display(brush);
    assertEquals("oval 0 10 50 100\n", brush.log());
}
```

Generally, spotting the possibility of an Imposter the first time requires insight. Ward Cunningham's insight that a vector of Moneys could act like a Money is just such a moment. You thought they were different, and now you can see them as being the same.

Following are two examples of Imposters that come up during refactoring:

- Null Object—You can treat the absence of data the same as the presence of data.

- Composite—You can treat a collection of objects the same as a single object.

Finding Imposters during refactoring is driven by eliminating duplication, just as all refactoring is driven by eliminating duplication.

Composite

How do you implement an object whose behavior is the composition of the behavior of a list of other objects? Make it an Imposter for the component objects.

My favorite example is also an example of the contradiction of Composites: Account and Transaction. Transactions store an increment of value (they are really a lot more complex and interesting, but for now . . .):

Transaction
```
Transaction(Money value) {
    this.value= value;
}
```

Accounts compute their balance by summing the values of their Transactions:

Account
```
Transaction transactions[];
Money balance() {
    Money sum= Money.zero();
    for (int i= 0; i < transactions.length; i++)
        sum= sum.plus(transactions[i].value);
    return sum;
}
```

It seems simple enough.

- Transactions have a value.

- Accounts have a balance.

Then comes the interesting part. A customer has a bunch of accounts and would like to see an overall balance. The obvious way to implement this is as a new class, OverallAccount, which sums the balances of a list of Accounts. Duplication! Duplication!

What if Account and Balance both implemented the same interface? Let's call it Holding because I can't think of anything better at the moment.

Holding
```
interface Holding
    Money balance();
```

Transactions can implement balance() by returning their value:

Transaction
```
Money balance() {
    return value;
}
```

Now Accounts can be composed of Holdings, not Transactions:

Account
```
Holding holdings[];
Money balance() {
```

```
    Money sum= Money.zero();
    for (int i= 0; i < holdings.length; i++)
        sum= sum.plus(holdings[i].balance());
    return sum;
}
```

Now our problem with OverallAccounts disappears. An OverallAccount is just an Account containing Accounts.

The smell of Composite is illustrated by the above. Transactions don't have balances, not in the real world. Applying Composite is a programmer's trick, not generally appreciated by the rest of the world. However, the benefits to program design are enormous, so the conceptual disconnect is often worth it. Folders containing Folders, TestSuites containing TestSuites, Drawings containing Drawings—none of these translate well from the world, but they all make the code so much simpler.

I had to play with Composite for a long time before I found where to use it and where not to use it. As is obvious from this discussion, I'm still not able to articulate how to guess when a collection of objects is just a collection of objects and when you really have a Composite. The good news is, since you're getting good at refactoring, the moment the duplication appears, you can introduce Composite and watch program complexity disappear.

Collecting Parameter

How do you collect the results of an operation that is spread over several objects? Add a parameter to the operation in which the results will be collected.

A simple example is the java.io.Externalizable interface. The writeExternal method writes an object and all the objects it references. Because the objects all have to cooperate loosely to get written out, the method is passed a parameter, an ObjectOutput, as the collecting parameter:

java.io.Externalizable
```
public interface Externalizable extends java.io.Serializable {
    void writeExternal(ObjectOutput out) throws IOException;
}
```

Adding a Collecting Parameter is a common consequence of Composite. In developing JUnit, we didn't need the TestResult to collate the results of several tests until we had several tests.

As the sophistication of expected results grows, you may find the need to introduce a Collecting Parameter. For example, suppose we are printing Expressions. If all we want is a flat string, then concatenation is sufficient:

```
testSumPrinting() {
    Sum sum= new Sum(Money.dollar(5), Money.franc(7));
    assertEquals("5 USD + 7 CHF", sum.toString());
}

String toString() {
    return augend + " + " + addend;
}
```

If we want the indented tree form of the expression, however, the code would look like this:

```
testSumPrinting() {
    Sum sum= new Sum(Money.dollar(5), Money.franc(7));
    assertEquals("+\n\t5 USD\n\t7 CHF", sum.toString());
}
```

We will have to introduce a Collecting Parameter, something like this:

```
String toString() {
    IndentingStream writer= new IndentingStream();
    toString(writer);
    return writer.contents();
}

void toString(IndentingWriter writer) {
    writer.println("+");
    writer.indent();
    augend.toString(writer);
    writer.println();
    addend.toString(writer);
    writer.exdent();
}
```

Singleton

How do you provide global variables in languages without global variables? Don't. Your programs will thank you for taking the time to think about design instead.

Chapter 31

Refactoring

These patterns describe how to change the design of the system, even radically, in small steps.

In TDD we use refactoring[1] in an interesting way. Usually, a refactoring cannot change the semantics of the program under any circumstances. In TDD, the circumstances we care about are the tests that are already passing. So, for example, we can replace constants with variables in TDD and, in good conscience, call this operation a refactoring, because it doesn't change the set of tests that pass. The only circumstance under which semantics are preserved may actually be our one test case. Any other test case that was passing would fail. However, we don't have those tests yet, so we don't worry about them.

This "observational equivalence" places a burden on you to have enough tests so that—as far as you know and at least by the time you're done—a refactoring with respect to the tests is the same as a refactoring with respect to all possible tests. It's no excuse to say, "I knew there was a problem, but the tests all passed so I checked the code in." Write more tests.

Reconcile Differences

How do you unify two similar looking pieces of code? Gradually bring them closer. Unify them only when they are absolutely identical.

Refactoring can be a nerve-wracking experience. The easy ones are obvious. If I extract a method and do so mechanically correctly, there is very little chance of changing the system's behavior. But some refactorings push you to examine the control flows and data values carefully. A long chain of reasoning leads you to believe that the change you are about to make won't change any answers. Those are the refactorings that enhance your hairline.

---

1. Fowler, Martin. 1999. *Refactoring: Improving the Design of Existing Code*. Boston: Addison-Wesley. ISBN 0201485672.

Such a leap-of-faith refactoring is exactly what we're trying to avoid with our strategy of small steps and concrete feedback. Although you can't always avoid leapy refactorings, you can reduce their incidence.

This refactoring occurs at all levels of scale.

- Two loop structures are similar. By making them identical, you can merge them.

- Two branches of a conditional are similar. By making them identical, you can eliminate the conditional.

- Two methods are similar. By making them identical, you can eliminate one.

- Two classes are similar. By making them identical, you can eliminate one.

Sometimes you need to approach reconciling differences backward—that is, think about how the last step of the change could be trivial, then work backward. For example, if you want to remove several subclasses, the trivial last step is if a subclass contains nothing. Then the superclass can replace the subclass without changing the behavior of the system. To empty out this subclass, this method needs to be made identical to the one in the superclass. One by one, empty out the subclasses and, when they are empty, replace references to them with references to the superclass.

Isolate Change

How do you change one part of a multi-part method or object? First, isolate the part that has to change.

The picture that comes to my mind is surgery: The entire patient except the part to be operated on is draped. The draping leaves the surgeon with only a fixed set of variables. Now, we could have long arguments over whether this abstraction of a person to a lower left quadrant abdomen leads to good health care, but at the moment of surgery, I'm kind of glad the surgeon can focus.

You may find that once you've isolated the change and then made the change, the result is so trivial that you can undo the isolation. If we found that really all we needed was to return the instance variable in findRate(), then we should consider inlining findRate() everywhere it is used and deleting it. Don't make these changes automatically, however. Balance the cost of an additional method with the value of having an additional concept explicit in the code.

Some possible ways to isolate change are Extract Method (the most common), Extract Object, and Method Object.

Migrate Data

How do you move from one representation? Temporarily duplicate the data.

How

Here is the internal-to-external version, in which you change the representation internally and then change the externally visible interface.

- Add an instance variable in the new format.

- Set the new format variable everywhere you set the old format.

- Use the new format variable everywhere you use the old format.

- Delete the old format.

- Change the external interface to reflect the new format.

Sometimes, however, you will want to change the API first. Then you should:

- Add a parameter in the new format.

- Translate from the new format parameter to the old format internal representation.

- Delete the old format parameter.

- Replace uses of the old format with the new format.

- Delete the old format.

Why

One to Many creates a data migration problem every time. Suppose we wanted to implement TestSuite using One to Many. We would start with:

```
def testSuite(self):
    suite= TestSuite()
    suite.add(WasRun("testMethod"))
    suite.run(self.result)
    assert("1 run, 0 failed" == self.result.summary())
```

which is implemented (in the "One" part of One to Many) by:

```
class TestSuite:
    def add(self, test):
        self.test= test
    def run(self, result):
        self.test.run(result)
```

Now we begin duplicating data. First we initialize the collection of tests:

TestSuite
```
def __init__(self):
    self.tests= []
```

Everywhere test is set, we add to the collection, too:

TestSuite
```
def add(self, test):
    self.test= test
    self.tests.append(test)
```

Now we use the list of tests instead of the single test. For purposes of the current test cases, this is a refactoring (it preserves semantics) because there is only ever one element in the collection.

TestSuite
```
def run(self, result):
    for test in self.tests:
        test.run(result)
```

We delete the now-unused instance variable test:

TestSuite
```
def add(self, test):
    self.tests.append(test)
```

You can also use stepwise data migration when moving between equivalent formats with different protocols, as in moving from Java's Vector/Enumerator to Collection/Iterator.

Extract Method

How do you make a long, complicated method easier to read? Turn a small part of it into a separate method and call the new method.

How

Extract Method is actually one of the more complicated atomic refactorings. I'll describe the typical case here. Fortunately, it is also the most commonly implemented automatic refactoring, so you're unlikely to have to do it by hand.

1. Find a region of the method that would make sense as its own method. Bodies of loop, whole loops, and branches of conditionals are common candidates for extraction.

2. Make sure that there are no assignments to temporary variables declared outside the scope of the region to be extracted.

3. Copy the code from the old method to the new method. Compile it.

4. For each temporary variable or parameter of the original method used in the new method, add a parameter to the new method.

5. Call the new method from the original method.

Why

I use Extract Method when I'm trying to understand complicated code. "Here, this bit here is doing something. What shall we call that?" After half an hour, the code is looking better, your partner realizes that you really *are* there to help, and you understand much better what is going on.

I use Extract Method to eliminate duplication when I see that two methods have some parts the same and some parts different. I extract out the similar bits as methods. (The Smalltalk Refactoring Browser even goes and checks to see if you are extracting a method that is equivalent to one you already have, and offers to use the existing method instead of creating a new one.)

Breaking methods into tiny bits can sometimes go too far. When I can no longer see a way forward, I often use Inline Method (conveniently, the next refactoring) to get all the code in one place so I can see what should be extracted anew.

Inline Method

How do you simplify control flows that have become too twisted or scattered? Replace a method invocation with the method itself.

How

1. Copy the method.

2. Paste the method over the method invocation.

3. Replace all formal parameters with actual parameters. If, for example, you pass reader.getNext() (an expression causing side effects), then be careful to assign it to a local variable.

Why

One of the reviewers of this book complained about the sequence in Part I where a Bank is asked to reduce an Expression to a single Money.

```
public void testSimpleAddition() {
    Money five= Money.dollar(5);
    Expression sum= five.plus(five);
    Bank bank= new Bank();
    Money reduced= bank.reduce(sum, "USD");
    assertEquals(Money.dollar(10), reduced);
}
```

"This is too complicated. Why don't you just ask the Money to reduce itself?" How do we experiment? Inline the implementation of Bank.reduce() and see what it looks like:

```
public void testSimpleAddition() {
    Money five= Money.dollar(5);
    Expression sum= five.plus(five);
    Bank bank= new Bank();
    Money reduced= sum.reduce(bank, "USD");
    assertEquals(Money.dollar(10), reduced);
}
```

You might like the second version better, or you might not. The point to note here is that you can use Inline Method to play around with the flow of control. When I'm refactoring, I have a mental picture of the system with bits of logic and control flow sloshing around between the objects. When I think I see something promising, I use the refactorings to try it out and see the result.

In the heat of battle I'll occasionally get caught up in my own cleverness. (I'm not going to say how often those occasions come.) When I do, Inline Method is a way for me to reel myself back in: "I have this sending to that, sending to that . . . Whoa, Nelly. What's going on here?" I inline a few layers of abstraction, see what's really going on, and then I can re-abstract the code according to its actual needs, not my preconceptions.

Extract Interface

How do you introduce a second implementation of operations in Java? Create an interface containing the shared operations.

How

1. Declare an interface. Sometimes the name of the existing class should be the name of the interface, in which case you should first rename the class.

2. Have the existing class implement the interface.

3. Add the necessary methods to the interface, expanding the visibility of the methods in the class if necessary.

4. Change type declarations from the class to the interface where possible.

Why

Sometimes when you need to extract an interface, you are genuinely moving from the first implementation to the second. You have a Rectangle and you want to add an Oval, so you create a Shape interface. Finding names for the interfaces in this case is generally easy, although sometimes you have to struggle to find the right metaphor.

Sometimes you are introducing a Crash Test Dummy or other Mock Object when you need to extract an interface. Naming is generally tougher in this case, because you still only have one real example. These are the times I'm most tempted to cop out and name the interface IFile and leave the class named File. I've schooled myself to stop a moment and see if I don't understand something deeper about what is going on. Perhaps the interface should be called File and the class DiskFile, because the class assumes that the bits are on a disk.

Move Method

How do you move a method to the place where it belongs? Add it to the class where it belongs, then invoke it.

How

1. Copy the method.

2. Paste the method, suitably named, into the target class. Compile it.

3. If the original object is referenced in the method, then add a parameter to pass the original object. If variables of the original object are referenced, then pass them as parameters. If variables of the original object are set, then you should give up.

4. Replace the body of the original method with an invocation of the new method.

How

This is one of my favorite consulting refactorings, because it is so good at uncovering unwarranted preconceptions. Calculating areas is the responsibility of the Shape:

Shape

```
...
int width= bounds.right() - bounds.left();
int height= bounds.bottom() - bounds.top();
int area= width * height;
...
```

Any time I see more than one message sent to another object in a method, I get suspicious. In this case, I see that bounds (a Rectangle) is being sent four messages. Time to move this part of the method:

Rectangle

```
public int area() {
    int width= this.right() - this.left();
    int height= this.bottom() - this.top();
    return width * height;
}
```

Shape

```
...
int area= bounds.area();
...
```

The three great properties of Move Method are as follows.

*   It's easy to see the need for it without deep understanding of the meaning of the code. You see two or more messages to a different object and away you go.

- The mechanics are quick and safe.

- The results are often enlightening. "But Rectangles don't do any calculation . . . Oh, I see. That *is* better."

Sometimes you will want to move only part of a method. You can first extract a method, move the whole method, then inline the (now one line) method in the original class. Or you can figure out the mechanics for doing it in one go.

Method Object

How do you represent a complicated method that requires several parameters and local variables? Make an object out of the method.

How

- Create an object with the same parameters as the method.

- Make the local variables also instance variables of the object.

- Create one method called run(), whose body is the same as the body of the original method.

- In the original method, create a new object and invoke run().

Why

Method Objects are useful in preparation for adding a whole new kind of logic to the system. For example, you might have several methods involved in computing the cash flow from component cash flows. When you want to start computing the net present value of the cash flows, you can first create a Method Object out of the first style of computation. Then you can write the new style of computation with its own, smaller scale, tests. Then plugging in the new style will be a single step.

Method Objects are also good for simplifying code that doesn't yield to Extract Method. Sometimes you'll find a block of code that has a bunch of temporary variables and parameters, and every time you try to extract a piece of it you have to carry along five or six temps and parameters. The resulting extracted method doesn't look any better than the original code, because the method signature is so long. Creating a Method Object gives you a new namespace in which you can extract methods without having to pass anything.

Add Parameter

How do you add a parameter to a method?

How

1. If the method is in an interface, add the parameter to the interface first.

2. Add the parameter.

3. Use the compiler errors to tell you what calling code you need to change.

Why

Adding a parameter is often an extension step. You got the first test case running without needing the parameter, but in this new circumstance you have to take more information into account in order to compute correctly.

Adding a parameter can also be part of migrating from one data representation to another. First you add the parameter, then you delete all uses of the old parameter, then you delete the old parameter.

Method Parameter to Constructor Parameter

How do you move a parameter from a method or methods to the constructor?

How

1. Add a parameter to the constructor.

2. Add an instance variable with the same name as the parameter.

3. Set the variable in the constructor.

4. One by one, convert references to "parameter" to "this.parameter".

5. When no more references exist to the parameter, delete the parameter from the method and all caller.

6. Remove the now-superfluous "this." from references.

7. Rename the variable correctly.

Why

If you pass the same parameter to several different methods in the same object, then you can simplify the API by passing the parameter once (eliminating duplication). You can run this refactoring in reverse if you find that an instance variable is used in only one method.

Chapter 32

Mastering TDD

I hope to raise questions here for you to ponder as you integrate TDD into your own practice. Some of the questions are small, and some are large. Sometimes the answers are here, or at least hinted at here, and sometimes the questions are left for you to explore.

How large should your steps be?

There are really two questions lurking here:

- How much ground should each test cover?

- How many intermediate stages should you go through as you refactor?

You could write the tests so they each encouraged the addition of a single line of logic and a handful of refactorings. You could write the tests so they each encouraged the addition of hundreds of lines of logic and hours of refactoring. Which should you do?

Part of the answer is that you should be able to do either. The tendency of Test-Driven Developers over time is clear, though—smaller steps. However, folks are experimenting with driving development from application-level tests, either alone or in conjunction with the programmer-level tests we've been writing.

At first when you refactor, you should be prepared to take lots of little tiny steps. Manual refactoring is prone to error, and the more errors you make and only catch later, the less likely you are to refactor. Once you've done a refactoring 20 times by hand in little tiny steps, experiment with leaving out some of the steps.

Automated refactoring accelerates refactoring enormously. What would have taken you 20 manual steps now becomes a single menu item. An order of magnitude change in quantity generally constitutes a change in quality, and this is true of automated refactoring. When you know you have the support of an excellent tool, you become much more aggressive in your refactorings, trying many more experiments to see how the code wants to be structured.

The Refactoring Browser for Smalltalk is as I write still the best refactoring tool available. Java refactoring support is appearing in many Java IDEs, and refactoring support is sure to spread quickly to other languages and environments.

What don't you have to test?

The simple answer, supplied by Phlip is, "Write tests until fear is transformed into boredom." This is a feedback loop, however, and it requires that you find the answer yourself. Because you came to this book for answers, not questions (in which case you're already reading the wrong section, but enough of the self-referential literary recursion stuff), try this list. You should test:

- Conditionals

- Loops

- Operations

- Polymorphism

But only those that you write. Unless you have reason to distrust it, don't test code from others. Sometimes, the precise specification of (by which I mean "bugs in") external code requires you to write more logic of your own. See above for whether you have to test this. Sometimes, just to be extra careful, I will document the presence of, um, unusual behavior in external code with a test that will fail if the bug is ever fixed, er, the behavior is ever refined.

How do you know if you have good tests?

The tests are a canary in a coal mine revealing by their distress the presence of evil design vapors. Here are some attributes of tests that suggest a design in trouble.

- Long setup code—If you have to spend a hundred lines creating the objects for one simple assertion, then something is wrong. Your objects are too big and need to be split.

- Setup duplication—If you can't easily find a common place for common setup code, then there are too many objects too tightly intertwined.

- Long running tests—TDD tests that run a long time won't be run often, and often haven't been run for a while, and probably don't work. Worse than this, they suggest that testing the bits and pieces of the application is hard. Difficulty testing bits and pieces is a design problem, and needs to be addressed with design. (The equivalent of 9.8 m/s^2 is the ten-minute test suite. Suites that take longer than ten minutes inevitably get trimmed, or the application tuned up, so the suite takes ten minutes again.)

- Fragile tests—Tests that break unexpectedly suggest that one part of the application is surprisingly affecting another part. You need to design until the effect at a distance is eliminated, either by breaking the connection or by bringing the two parts together.

How does TDD lead to frameworks?

Paradox: by not considering the future of your code, you make your code much more likely to be adaptable in the future.

I learned exactly the opposite from books: "Code for today, design for tomorrow." TDD appears to stand this advice on its head: "Code for tomorrow, design for today." Here's what happens in practice.

- The first feature goes in. It is implemented simply and straightforwardly, so it is done quickly and with few defects.

- The second feature, a variation on the first, goes in. The duplication between the two features is put in one place, whereas the differences tend to go in different places (different methods or even different classes).

- The third feature, a variation on the first two, goes in. The common logic is likely to be reusable as is, perhaps with a few tweaks. The unique logic tends to have an obvious home, either in a different method or a different class.

The Open/Closed Principle (objects should be open for use and closed to further modification) is gradually satisfied, and for precisely those kinds of variation that occur in practice. Test driving development leaves you with frameworks that are good at expressing exactly the kind of variation that occurs, even though the frameworks might not be good at expressing the kind of variation that doesn't occur (or hasn't occurred yet).

So, what happens when an unusual variation pops up three years later? The design undergoes rapid evolution in exactly the necessary spots to accommodate the variation. The Open/Closed Principle is violated, just for a moment, but the violation is not all that costly because you have all those tests to give you confidence you aren't breaking anything.

At the limit, where you introduce the variations very quickly, TDD is indistinguishable from designing ahead. I grew a reporting framework once over the course of a few hours, and observers were absolutely certain it was a trick. I must have started with the resulting framework in mind. No, sorry. I've just been test driving development long enough that I can recover from most of my mistakes faster than you can recognize I've made them.

How much feedback do you need?

How many tests should you write? Here's a simple problem: given three integers representing the length of the sides of a triangle, return:

- 1 if the triangle is equilateral

- 2 if the triangle is isosceles

- 3 if the triangle is scalene

and throw an exception if the triangle is not well formed.

Go ahead, try the problem (my Smalltalk solution is listed at the end of this question).

I wrote six tests (kind of like "Name That Tune": "I can code that problem in four tests." "Code that problem.") Bob Binder, in his comprehensive book *Testing Object-Oriented Systems*,[1] wrote 65 for the same problem. You'll have to decide, from experience and reflection, about how many tests you want to write.

I think about Mean Time Between Failures (MTBF) when I think about how many tests to write. For example, Smalltalk integers act like integers, not like a 32-bit counter, so it doesn't make sense to test MAXINT. Well, there is a maximum size for an integer, but it has to do with how much memory you have. Do I need to write a test that fills up memory with extremely large integers? How will that affect the MTBF of my program? If I'm never going to get anywhere close to that size of triangle, my program is not measurably more robust with such a test than without it.

Whether a test makes sense to write depends on how carefully you measure MTBF. If you are trying to get from an MTBF of 10 years to an MTBF of 100 years in your pacemaker, then tests for extremely unlikely conditions and com-

1. Binder, Bob. 1999. *Testing Object-Oriented Systems: Models, Patterns, and Tools.* Boston: Addison-Wesley. ISBN 0201809389. This is *the* comprehensive reference on testing.

binations of conditions make sense, unless you can demonstrate in some other way that the conditions cannot arise.

TDD's view of testing is pragmatic. In TDD, the tests are a means to an end—the end being code in which we have great confidence. If our knowledge of the implementation gives us confidence even without a test, then we will not write that test. Black box testing, where we deliberately choose to ignore the implementation, has some advantages. By ignoring the code, it demonstrates a different value system—the tests are valuable alone. It's an appropriate attitude to take in some circumstances, but that is different from TDD.

TriangleTest

```
testEquilateral
    self assert: (self evaluate: 2 side: 2 side: 2) = 1

testIsosceles
    self assert: (self evaluate: 1 side: 2 side: 2) = 2

testScalene
    self assert: (self evaluate: 2 side: 3 side: 4) = 3

testIrrational
    [self evaluate: 1 side: 2 side: 3]
        on: Exception
        do: [:ex | ^self].
    self fail

testNegative
    [self evaluate: -1 side: 2 side: 2]
        on: Exception
        do: [:ex | ^self].
    self fail

testStrings
    [self evaluate: 'a' side: 'b' side: 'c']
        on: Exception
        do: [:ex | ^self].
    self fail

evaluate: aNumber1 side: aNumber2 side: aNumber3
    | sides |
    sides := SortedCollection
        with: aNumber1
        with: aNumber2
        with: aNumber3.
    sides first <= 0 ifTrue: [self fail].
    (sides at: 1) + (sides at: 2) <= (sides at: 3) ifTrue: [self fail].
    ^sides asSet size
```

When should you delete tests?

More tests are better, but if two tests are redundant with respect to each other, should you keep them both around? That depends on two criteria.

- The first criterion for your tests is confidence. Never delete a test if it reduces your confidence in the behavior of the system.

- The second criterion is communication. If you have two tests that exercise the same path through the code, but they speak to different scenarios for a reader, leave them alone.

That said, if you have two tests that are redundant with respect to confidence and communication, delete the least useful of the two.

How do the programming language and environment influence TDD?

Try TDD in Smalltalk with the Refactoring Browser. Try it in C++ with vi. How does your experience differ?

In programming languages and environments where TDD cycles (test/compile/run/refactor) are harder to come by, you will likely be tempted to take larger steps:

- Cover more ground with each test.

- Refactor with fewer intermediate steps.

Does this make you go faster or slower?

In programming languages and environments where TDD cycles are plentiful, you will likely be tempted to try lots more experiments. Does this help you go faster or reach better solutions, or would you be better off institutionalizing some kind of time for pure reflection (reviews or literate programs)?

Can you test drive enormous systems?

Does TDD scale to extremely large systems? What new tests would you have to write? What new kinds of refactorings would you need?

The largest, totally test-driven system I've been involved with is at LifeWare (www.lifeware.ch). After 4 years and 40 person/years, the system contains approximately 250,000 lines of functional code and 250,000 lines of test code in Smalltalk. There are 4,000 tests, executing in under 20 minutes. The full suite is run several times each day. The amount of functionality in the system seems to have no bearing on the effectiveness of TDD. By eliminating duplication, you tend to create more smaller objects, and those objects can be tested in isolation independent of the size of the application.

Can you drive development with application-level tests?

The problem with driving development with small-scale tests (I call them "unit tests," but they don't match the accepted definition of unit tests very well) is that you run the risk of implementing what you think users want, but having it turn out not to be what they wanted at all. What if we wrote the tests at the level of the application? Then the users (with help) could write tests themselves for exactly what they wanted the system to do next.

There is a technical problem—fixturing. How can you write and run a test for a feature that doesn't exist yet? There always seems to be some way out of this problem, typically by introducing an interpreter which gracefully signals an error when it comes across a test that it doesn't know how to interpret yet.

There is also a social problem with application test-driven development (ATDD). Writing tests is a new responsibility for users (by which I really mean a team that includes users), and that responsibility comes at a new place in the development cycle—namely, before implementation begins. Organizations resist this kind of shift of responsibility. It will require concerted effort (that is, the effort of many people on the team working in concert) to get application tests written first.

TDD as described in this book is a technique that is entirely under your control. You can pick it up and start using it today if you so choose. Mixing up the rhythm of red/green/refactor, the technical issues of application fixturing, and the organizational change issues surrounding user-written tests is unlikely to be successful. The One Step Test rule applies. Get red/green/refactor going in your own practice, then spread the message.

Another aspect of ATDD is the length of the cycle between test and feedback. If a customer wrote a test and ten days later it finally worked, you would be staring at a red bar most of the time. I think I would still want to do programmer-level TDD, so that

- I got immediate green bars
- I simplified the internal design

How do you switch to TDD midstream?

You have a bunch of code that more or less works. You want to test drive your new code. What do you do next?

There is a whole book (or books) to be written about switching to TDD when you have lots of code. What follows is necessarily only a teaser.

The biggest problem is that code that isn't written with tests in mind typically isn't very testable. The interfaces aren't designed, so it is easy for you to isolate a little piece of logic, run it, and check its results.

"Fix it," you say. Yes, well, but refactoring (without automated tools) is likely to result in errors, errors that you won't catch because you don't have the tests. Chickens and eggs. Catch-22. Mutually assured destruction. What do you do?

What you don't do is go write tests for the whole thing and refactor the whole thing. That would take months, months in which no new functionality would appear. Spending money without making it is generally speaking not a sustainable process.

So first we have to decide to limit the scope of our changes. If we see parts of the system that could be dramatically simplified but that don't demand change at the moment, then we will leave them alone. Shed a tear, perhaps, for the sins of the past, but leave them alone.

Second, we have to break the deadlock between tests and refactoring. We can get feedback other ways than with tests, like working very carefully and with a partner. We can get feedback at a gross level, like system-level tests that we know aren't adequate but give us some confidence. With this feedback, we can make the areas we have to change more accepting of change.

Over time, the parts of the system that change all the time will come to look test driven. Occasionally we will wander into an unlit back alley and get mugged for our troubles, reminding us how slow things used to be. Then we will slow down, break the deadlock, and get going again.

Who is TDD intended for?

Every programming practice encodes a value system, explicitly or implicitly. TDD is no different. If you're happy slamming some code together that more or less works and you're happy never looking at the result again, TDD is not for you. TDD rests on a charmingly naïve geekoid assumption that if you write better code, you'll be more successful. TDD helps you to pay attention to the right issues at the right time so you can make your designs cleaner, you can refine your designs as you learn.

I say "naïve," but that's perhaps overstating. What's naïve is assuming that clean code is all there is to success. Good engineering is maybe 20 percent of a project's success. Bad engineering will certainly sink projects, but modest engineering can enable project success as long as the other 80 percent lines up right.

From this perspective, TDD is overkill. It lets you write code with far fewer defects and a much cleaner design than is common in the industry. However, those whose souls are healed by the balm of elegance can find in TDD a way to do well by doing good.

TDD is also good for geeks who form emotional attachments to code. One of the great frustrations of my young engineer's life was starting a project with great excitement, then watching the code base decay over time. A year later I wanted nothing more than to dump the now-smelly code and get on to the next project. TDD enables you to gain confidence in the code over time. As tests accumulate (and your testing improves), you gain confidence in the behavior of the system. As you refine the design, more and more changes become possible. My goal is to feel better about a project after a year than I did in the starry-eyed beginning, and TDD helps me achieve this.

Is TDD sensitive to initial conditions?

A certain order in which you take the tests seem to work very smoothly. Red/green/refactor/red/green/refactor. You can take the same tests and implement them in a different order, and it seems like there is not a way to advance in small steps. Is it really true that one sequence of tests is an order of magnitude faster/easier to implement than another? Is this just because my implementation technique is not up to the challenge? Is there something about the tests that should tell me to tackle them in a certain order? If TDD is sensitive to initial conditions in the small, then is it predictable in the large? (In the same way that little eddies in the Mississippi are unpredictable, but you can count on 2,000,000 cubic feet per second, more or less, at the river mouth.)

How does TDD relate to patterns?

All of my technical writings have been about trying to find fundamental rules that generate behavior similar to that of experts. In part, that's because this is how I learn—I find an expert to act like, then gradually figure out what is really going on. I'm certainly not looking for rules to be followed mechanically, although that is how the mechanically minded have interpreted them.

My oldest daughter (Hi Bethany! I told you I would get you in here—be glad it isn't more embarrassing) spent several years learning to do multiplication fast. My wife and I both prided ourselves on doing multiplication fast, and learned very quickly. What was going on? Turns out that every time Bethany was faced with 6 x 9, she would add 6, 9 times (or 9, 6 times, I suppose). Far from being a slow multiplier, she was a really fast adder.

The effect that I have noticed, and which I hope others find, is that by reducing repeatable behavior to rules, applying the rules becomes rote and mechanical. This is quicker than redebating everything from first principles all the time. When along comes an exception, or a problem that just doesn't fit any of the rules, you have more time and energy to generate and apply creativity.

This happened to me when writing the Smalltalk Best Practice Patterns. At some point I decided just to follow the rules I was writing. It was much slower at first, to be looking up the rules, or to be stopping to write a new rule. After a week, however, I discovered that code was ripping off my fingertips that would have required a pause for thought before. This gave me more time and attention for bigger thoughts about design and analysis.

Another relationship between TDD and patterns is TDD as an implementation method for pattern-driven design. Say we decide we want a Strategy for something. We write a test for the first variant and implement it as a method. Then we consciously write a test for the second variant, expecting the refactoring phase to drive us to a Strategy. Robert Martin and I did some research into this style of TDD. The problem is that the design keeps surprising you. Perfectly sensible design ideas turn out to be wrong. Better just to think about what you want the system to do, and let the design sort itself out later.

Why does TDD work?

Prepare to leave the galaxy. Let's assume for the moment that TDD helps teams productively build loosely coupled, highly cohesive systems with low defect rates and low cost maintenance profiles. (I'm claiming no such thing in general, but I trust you to imagine impossible things.) How could such a thing happen?

Part of the effect certainly comes from reducing defects. The sooner you find and fix a defect, the cheaper it is, often dramatically so (just ask the Mars Lander). There are plenty of secondary psychological and social effects from reduced defects. My own practice of programming became much less stressful when I started with TDD. No longer did I have to worry about everything at once. I could make this test run, and then all the rest. Relationships with my teammates became more positive. I stopped breaking builds, and people could rely on my software to work. Customers of my systems became more positive, too. A new release of the system just meant more functionality, not a host of new defects to identify among all of their old favorite bugs.

Reduced defects. Where do I get off claiming such a thing? Do I have scientific proof?

No. No studies have categorically demonstrated the difference between TDD and any of the many alternatives in quality, productivity, or fun. However, the anecdotal evidence is overwhelming, and the secondary effects are unmistakable. Programmers really do relax, teams really do develop trust, and customers really do learn to look forward to new releases. "By and large," I will say, although I haven't seen the opposite effect. Your mileage may vary, but you'll have to try it to find out.

Another advantage of TDD that may explain its effect is the way it shortens the feedback loop on design decisions. The feedback loop for implementation decisions is obviously short—seconds or minutes, followed by rerunning the tests tens or hundreds of times a day. The loop for design decisions goes between the design thought—perhaps the API should like this, or perhaps the metaphor should be that—and the first example, a test that embodies that thought. Rather than designing and then waiting weeks or months for someone else to feel the pain or glory, feedback comes in seconds or minutes as you try to translate your ideas into a plausible interface.

A weirder answer to, "Why does TDD work?" comes from the fevered imagination of complex systems. The inimitable Phlip says:

> Adopt programming practices that "attract" correct code as a limit function, not as an absolute value. If you write unit tests for every feature, and if you refactor to simplify code between each step, and if you add features one at a time and only after all the unit tests pass, you will create what mathematicians call an "attractor." This is a point in a state space that all flows converge on. Code is more likely to change for the better over time instead of for the worse; the attractor approaches correctness as a limit function.
>
> This is the "correctness" that nearly all programmers get by with (except, of course, for medical or aerospace software). But it's better to explicitly understand the attractor concept than deny it or disregard its importance.

What's with the name?

- Development—The old "phasist" way of thinking about software development is weakened because feedback between decisions is difficult if they are separated in time. Development in this sense means a complex dance of analysis, logical design, physical design, implementation, testing, review, integration, and deployment.

- Driven—I used to call TDD "test-first programming." However, the opposite of "first" is "last," and lots of people test after they have programmed. There is a naming rule that the opposite of a name should be at least vaguely unsatisfactory. (Part of the appeal of structured programming is that no one wants to be unstructured.) If you don't drive development with tests, what do you drive it with? Speculation? Specifications? (Ever notice that those two words come from the same root?)

- Test—Automated, reified, concrete tests. Push a button and they run. One of the ironies of TDD is that it isn't a testing technique (the Cunningham Koan). It's an analysis technique, a design technique, really a technique for structuring all the activities of development.

How does TDD relate to the practices of Extreme Programming?

Some reviewers of this book were concerned that by my writing a book exclusively about TDD, folks will take it as an excuse to ignore the rest of the advice in Extreme Programming (XP). For example, if you test drive, do you still need to pair? Here is a brief summary of how the rest of XP enhances TDD, and TDD enhances the rest of XP.

- Pairing—The tests you write in TDD are excellent conversation pieces when you are pairing. The problem you avoid is that of the partners not agreeing on what problem they are solving, even though they are trying to work on the same code. This sounds crazy, but it happens all the time, especially when you are learning to pair with someone. Pairing enhances TDD by giving you a fresh mind to take over when you get tired. TDD's rhythm can suck you in, and lead you to continue to program even when you're tired. Your partner, however, is ready to take the keyboard when you flag.

- Work fresh—On a related note, XP advises you to work when you are fresh and stop when you are tired. When you can't get that next test to work, or those two tests to work together, it's time for a break. Uncle Bob Martin and I were working on a line break algorithm once, and we just couldn't get it to work. We struggled in frustration for a few minutes, but it was obvious we weren't making progress, so we stopped.

- Continuous integration—The tests make an excellent resource, enabling you to integrate more often. You get another test working and the duplication removed, and you check in. The cycle can be 15 to 30 minutes instead of the 1 to 2 hours that I usually shoot for. This may be part of the key to having larger teams of programmers on the same code base. As Bill Wake says, "An n^2 problem is not a problem if n is always 1."

- Simple design—By coding only what you need for the tests and removing all duplication, you automatically get a design that is perfectly adapted to the current requirements and equally prepared for all future stories. The mind-set that you are looking for just enough design to have the perfect architecture for the current system also makes writing the tests easier.

- Refactoring—The Remove Duplication rule is another way of saying "refactoring." But the tests give you confidence that your larger refactorings haven't changed the behavior of the system. The higher your confidence, the more aggressive you will be in trying large-scale refactorings that extend the life of your system. By refactoring, you make writing the next round of tests that much easier.

- Continuous delivery—If TDD tests really do improve the MTBF of your system (a contention you will have to verify for yourself), then you can put code into production much more often without disrupting customers. Gareth Reeves makes the analogy to day trading. In day trading, you close out your positions every night, because you don't take risk around that which you aren't managing. In programming, you like all of your changes in production because you don't want code around that you aren't receiving concrete feedback on.

Darach's Challenge

Darach Ennis has thrown down a gauntlet for extending the reach of TDD. He says:

> There are a lot of fallacies blowing around various engineering organizations and amongst various engineers that this book could help to dispel and some of these are:
>
> - You can't test GUIs automatically (e.g., Swing, CGI, JSP/Servlets/Struts)
> - You can't unit test distributed objects automatically (e.g., RPC and Messaging style, or CORBA/EJB and JMS)
> - You can't test-first develop your database schema (e.g., JDBC)
> - There is no need to test third party code or code generated by external tools
> - You can't test first develop a language compiler / interpreter from BNF to production quality implementation

I'm not sure he's right, but I'm also not sure he's wrong. He's given me something to chew on as I think about how far to push TDD.

Appendix I

Influence Diagrams

This book contains many examples of influence diagrams. The idea of influence diagrams is taken from Gerald Weinberg's excellent *Quality Software Management* series, particularly Book 1: *Systems Thinking*.[1] The purpose of an influence diagram is to see how the elements of a system affect one another.

Influence diagrams have three elements:

- Activities, notated as a word or short phrase

- Positive connections, notated as a directed arrow between two activities; meaning that more of the source activity tends to create more of the destination activity, or less of the source activity tends to create less of the destination activity

- Negative connections, notated as a directed arrow between two activities with a circle over it; meaning that more of the source activity tends to create less of the destination activity, or less of the source activity tends to create more of the destination activity

A lot of words for a simple concept. Figures A.1 to A.3 provide a few examples.

The more I eat, the more I weigh. The less I eat, the less I weigh. Personal weight is a far more complicated system than this, of course. Influence diagrams are models to help you understand some aspect of the system, not understand and control it perfectly.

---

1. Weinberg, Gerald. 1992. *Systems Thinking. Quality Software Management*. New York: Dorset House. ISBN: 0932633226.

Circus
Attendance

Hedge Trimming

Figure A.1 *Two seemingly unrelated activities*

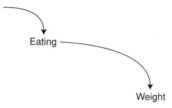

Figure A.2 *Positively connected activities*

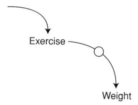

Figure A.3 *Negatively connected activities*

Feedback

Influence doesn't work in one direction only. Often the effects of an activity come back around to change the activity itself, either positively or negatively, as shown in Figure A.4.

If my weight rises, then my self-esteem drops, which makes we want to eat more, which makes my weight rise, and so on. Anytime you have a cycle in an influence diagram, you have feedback.

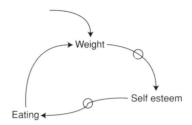

Figure A.4 *Feedback*

There are two kinds of feedback—positive and negative. Positive feedback causes systems to encourage more and more of an activity. You can find positive feedback loops by counting the number of negative connections in a cycle. If there are an even number of negative connections, then you have a positive feedback loop. The feedback loop in Figure A.4 is a positive feedback loop. It will cause you to keep gaining weight until the influence of some other activity kicks in.

Negative feedback damps or reduces an activity. Cycles with an odd number of negative connections are negative feedback loops.

The keys to system design are

- Creating virtuous cycles, in which positive feedback loops encourage the growth of good activities

- Avoiding death spirals, in which positive feedback loops encourage the growth of unproductive or destructive activities

- Creating negative feedback cycles to prevent overuse of good activities

System Control

When choosing a system of software development practices, you'd like the practices to support one another so that you tend to do about the right amount of any activity, even under stress. Figure A.5 is an example of a system of practices that leads to insufficient testing.

Under the pressure of time, you reduce the amount of testing, which increases the number of errors, which increases the time pressure. Eventually some outside activity (like "Cash Flow Panic") steps in to ship the software regardless.

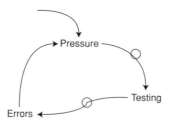

Figure A.5 *Not enough time to test reduces the available time*

When you have a system that isn't behaving, you do have options.

- Drive a positive feedback loop the other direction. If you have a loop between tests and confidence, and tests have been failing thus reducing confidence, then you can make more tests work to increase confidence in your ability to get more tests working.

- Introduce a negative feedback loop to control an activity that has grown too large.

- Create or break connections to eliminate loops that are not helping.

Appendix II

Fibonacci

In answer to a question from one of the reviewers of this book, I posted a test-driven Fibonacci. Several reviewers commented that this example turned on their light about how TDD works. However, it is not long enough, nor does it demonstrate enough of TDD techniques, to replace the existing examples. If your lights are still dark after reading the main examples, take a look here and see.

The first test shows that fib(0) = 0. The implementation returns a constant.

```
public void testFibonacci() {
    assertEquals(0, fib(0));
}

int fib(int n) {
    return 0;
}
```

(I am just using the TestCase class as a home for the code, because it is only a single function.)

The second test shows that fib(1) = 1.

```
public void testFibonacci() {
    assertEquals(0, fib(0));
    assertEquals(1, fib(1));
}
```

I just put the second assert in the same method, because there didn't seem to be any substantial communication value to writing testFibonacciOfOneIsOne.

There are several ways I could go to make this run. I'll choose to treat 0 as a special case:

```
int fib(int n) {
    if (n == 0) return 0;
    return 1;
}
```

The duplication in the test case is starting to bug me, and it will only get worse as we add new cases. We can factor out the common structure of the assertions by driving the test from a table of input and expected values.

```
public void testFibonacci() {
    int cases[][]= {{0,0},{1,1}};
    for (int i= 0; i < cases.length; i++)
        assertEquals(cases[i][1], fib(cases[i][0]));
}
```

Now adding the next case requires six keystrokes and no additional lines:

```
public void testFibonacci() {
    int cases[][]= {{0,0},{1,1},{2,1}};
    for (int i= 0; i < cases.length; i++)
        assertEquals(cases[i][1], fib(cases[i][0]));
}
```

Disconcertingly, the test works. It just so happens that our constant 1 is right for this case as well. On to the next test:

```
public void testFibonacci() {
    int cases[][]= {{0,0},{1,1},{2,1},{3,2}};
    for (int i= 0; i < cases.length; i++)
        assertEquals(cases[i][1], fib(cases[i][0]));
}
```

Hooray, it fails. Applying the same strategy as before (treating smaller inputs as special cases), we write:

```
int fib(int n) {
    if (n == 0) return 0;
    if (n <= 2) return 1;
    return 2;
}
```

Now we are ready to generalize. We wrote 2, but we don't really mean 2, we mean 1 + 1.

```
int fib(int n) {
    if (n == 0) return 0;
    if (n <= 2) return 1;
    return 1 + 1;
}
```

That first 1 is an example of fib(n-1):

```
int fib(int n) {
    if (n == 0) return 0;
    if (n <= 2) return 1;
    return fib(n-1) + 1;
}
```

The second 1 is an example of fib(n-2):

```
int fib(int n) {
   if (n == 0) return 0;
   if (n <= 2) return 1;
   return fib(n-1) + fib(n-2);
}
```

Cleaning up now, the same structure should work for fib(2), so we can tighten up the second condition:

```
int fib(int n) {
   if (n == 0) return 0;
   if (n == 1) return 1;
   return fib(n-1) + fib(n-2);
}
```

And there we have Fibonacci, derived totally from the tests.

Afterword

One of the hardest things to communicate about test-driven development is the mental state that it puts you in. I remember a session on the original C3 project with Ralph Beattie where we had to implement a complicated set of pay conditions. Ralph broke them down into a set of test cases, and off we set one by one to make them work. Progress was steady and unhurried; because it was unhurried it seemed slow, but looking back on how much we got done, it was clear that despite the unhurried feeling progress was really fast.

Despite all the fancy tools that we have, programming is still hard. I can remember many programming times when I feel like I was trying to keep several balls in the air at once, any lapse of concentration and everything would come tumbling down. Test-driven development helps reduce that feeling, and as a result you get this rapid unhurriedness.

I think the reason for this is that working in a test-driven development style gives you this sense of keeping just one ball in the air at once, so you can concentrate on that ball properly and do a really good job with it. When I'm trying to add some new functionality, I'm not worried about what really makes a good design for this piece of function, I'm just trying to get a test to pass as easily as I can. When I switch to refactoring mode, I'm not worried about adding some new function, I'm just worried about getting the right design. With both of these I'm just focused on one thing at a time, and as a result I can concentrate better on that one thing.

Adding features test-first and refactoring are two of these monological flavors of programming. At a recent stint at the keyboard I experienced another one: pattern copying. I was writing a little Ruby script that pulled some data out of a database. As I did this I started on a class to wrap the database table and thought to myself that since I'd just finished off a book of database patterns I should use a pattern. Although the sample code was Java, it wasn't difficult to adapt it to Ruby. While I programmed it I didn't really think about the problem, I just thought about making a fair adaptation of the pattern to the language and specific data I was manipulating.

Pattern copying on its own isn't good programming—a fact I always stress when talking about patterns. Patterns are always half baked, and need to be adapted in the oven of your own project. But a good way to do this is to first copy the pattern fairly blindly, and then use some mix of refactoring or test-first, to perform the adaptation. That way when you're doing the pattern-copying, you can concentrate on just the pattern—one thing at a time.

The XP community has struggled with where patterns fit into the picture. Clearly the XP community is in favor of patterns, after all there is huge intersection between XP advocates and patterns advocates—Ward and Kent were leaders in both. Perhaps pattern copying is a third monological mode to go with test-first and refactoring, and like those two is dangerous on its own but powerful in concert.

A large part making activities systematic is identifying core tasks and allowing us to concentrate on only one at a time. An assembly line is a mind-numbing example of this—mind numbing because you always do the one thing. Perhaps what test-driven development suggests is a way of breaking apart the act of programming into elemental modes, but avoiding the monotony by switching rapidly between those modes. The combination of monological modes and switching gives you the benefits of focus and lowers the stress on the brain without the monotony of the assembly line.

I'll admit these thoughts are somewhat half-baked. As I write this I'm still unsure if I believe what I say, and I know I'll be mulling over these thoughts over a few, or many months. But I thought you might like them anyway, perhaps to stimulate your thoughts on the bigger picture that test-first development fits into. It's not a picture that we see clearly yet, but it's one I think is slowly revealing itself.

Index

217